DK EYEWITNESS

TOP 10
MIAMI
AND THE KEYS

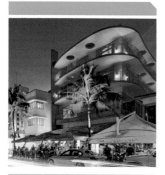

Top 10 Miami and the Keys Highlights

The Top 10 of Everything

Welcome to Miami
and the Keys **5**

Exploring Miami and the Keys **6**

Miami and the Keys
Highlights **10**

South Beach **12**

Art Deco District **14**

Calle Ocho, Little Havana **18**

Vizcaya Museum
and Gardens **20**

Merrick's Coral Gables
Fantasies **24**

Lowe Art Museum **26**

The Wolfsonian–FIU **28**

Gold Coast **30**

Key West **32**

The Everglades **34**

Historic Sites
and Monuments **38**

Architectural Wonders **40**

Museums **42**

Romantic Spots **44**

Spots for People-Watching **46**

Parks and Gardens **48**

Beaches **50**

Sports and Outdoor Activities **52**

Snorkeling and Diving **54**

Off the Beaten Path **56**

Children's Attractions **58**

Performing Arts Venues **60**

LGBTQ+ Venues **62**

Nightlife **64**

Restaurants **66**

Chic Shopping Centers **68**

Malls and Markets **70**

Miami and the Keys for Free **72**

Festivals **74**

Walks, Drives, and
Cycling Routes **76**

CONTENTS

Miami and the Keys Area by Area

Miami Beach and
  Key Biscayne **80**

Downtown and Little Havana **90**

North of Downtown.....................**98**

Coral Gables and
  Coconut Grove **106**

South of Coconut Grove.............**114**

The Keys....................................**120**

Side Trips..................................**132**

Streetsmart

Getting Around **140**

Practical Information................**144**

Places to Stay............................**148**

General Index............................**154**

Acknowledgments **159**

Within each Top 10 list in this book, no hierarchy of quality or popularity is implied. All 10 are, in the editor's opinion, of roughly equal merit.

Throughout this book, floors are referred to in accordance with American usage; i.e., the "first floor" is at ground level.

Title page, front cover and spine *The iconic Colony Hotel in South Beach's hip Art Deco District*

Back cover, clockwise from top left *A bright Flamingo head; diners on Ocean Drive; a busy street in Collins Avenue; Art Deco District; Miami Beach lined with palm trees*

The rapid rate at which the world is changing is constantly keeping the DK Eyewitness team on our toes. While we've worked hard to ensure that this edition of Miami and the Keys is accurate and up-to-date, we know that opening hours alter, standards shift, prices fluctuate, places close and new ones pop up in their stead. So, if you notice we've got something wrong or left something out, we want to hear about it. Please get in touch at **travelguides@dk.com**

Welcome to
Miami and the Keys

With its world-class beaches, Art Deco architecture, and pulsating nightlife, Miami is Florida's most glamorous city. Home to a sizeable Latin American population, the city also has a robust and varied cultural scene. To the south, the Keys are a string of reef-fringed islands, sprinkled with white-sand beaches culminating at Key West. With DK Eyewitness Top 10 Miami and the Keys, it's yours to explore.

Miami's hedonistic heart is **South Beach**: trendy and stylish, with fine dining and fashionable shopping. Everything ultimately revolves around the beach itself, an enticing stretch of sand backed by hip hotels. The skyscrapers of **Downtown** Miami, by contrast, harbor historic sights and intriguing museums, while nearby **Little Havana** is the hub of everything Cuban, from traditional fruit-juice stalls to cigar factories. North of Downtown lie the **Wynwood murals**, the trendy stores of the **Design District**, and **Little Haiti**, one of the city's most exuberant areas.

Meanwhile, at Florida's southern tip, the **Keys** are an archipelago of over 10,000 tiny islands of which fewer than 50 are inhabited. Just offshore lies the Florida Reef, a great wall of living coral with a dazzling array of marine life. **Key West** is home to museums and **The Hemingway Home**, lively bars, and spectacular sunsets.

Whether you're coming for a weekend or a week, our Top 10 guide brings together the best of everything the region has to offer, from hip South Beach to traditional Cuban diners. The guide has useful tips throughout, from seeking out what's free to places off the beaten path, plus nine easy-to-follow itineraries designed to tie together a clutch of sights in a short space of time. Add inspiring photography and detailed maps, and you've got the essential pocket-sized travel companion. **Enjoy the book, and enjoy Miami and the Keys**.

Clockwise from top: Bahia Honda State Park, Atlantic coral reef at Key Largo, Ocean Drive, Miami skyline, Art Deco fountain, tearoom at Vizcaya museum, Sloppy Joe's bar at Key West

Exploring Miami and the Keys

There are so many things to do in Miami and the Keys, you could easily spend a couple of weeks here. Whether you're visiting for a weekend or have the luxury of an extra couple of days, these two- and four-day itineraries will help you make the most of your time.

The Biscayne Bay boat tour is a very popular way of seeing the sights.

Two Days in Miami

Day ❶
MORNING
Begin by having breakfast at **Bayside Marketplace** *(see p92)*, followed by a boat tour of Biscayne Bay *(see p59)*. Afterwards stroll to Downtown Miami, taking in the exhibits and gardens at the **Pérez Art Museum** *(see p91)*.

AFTERNOON
Head to **South Beach** *(see pp12–13)* for lunch on the seafront, before soaking up the Art Deco heritage along Collins and Washington avenues. Be sure to make time for the **Wolfsonian–FIU** *(see pp28–9)* and **Lincoln Road Mall** *(see p82)*, before getting back to the beach for dinner and to soak up the **South Beach nightlife** *(see p87)*.

Day ❷
MORNING
Start the day in **Little Havana** *(see pp18–19)* for a traditional Cuban breakfast at **Versailles** *(see p97)*. Visit the Little Havana Cigar Factory *(see p19)* and the Calle Ocho Walk of Fame *(see p19)* before touring the **Vizcaya Museum and Gardens** *(see pp20–21)*.

Key

— Two-day itinerary
— Four-day itinerary

Mahoga Hammock Tr

Everglaa National Pa

Key West

④

Bahia Honda State Park

AFTERNOON
Take a tour of **Coral Gables** *(see pp24–5)*, before checking out the work at the **Lowe Art Museum** *(see pp26–7)*. End the day with dinner at **The Biltmore** *(see p24)*.

Four Days in Miami and the Keys

Day ❶
MORNING
Sample **South Beach** *(see pp12–13)* life with breakfast at a café on **Ocean Drive**, then wander along Collins and Washington avenues to admire the **Art Deco District** *(see pp14–17)*, stopping at the

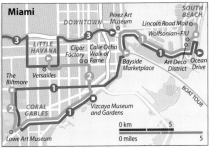

Wolfsonian–FIU *(see pp28–9)*. Head to Coral Gables for lunch at **The Biltmore** *(see p24)*.

AFTERNOON

After lunch take in some of George Merrick's fabulous architecture around **Coral Gables** *(see pp24–5)*, and the exhibits at the **Lowe Art Museum** *(see pp26–7)*. End the day with a tour of the **Vizcaya Museum and Gardens** *(see pp20–21)*.

Day ❷

MORNING

Spend the day exploring the **Gold Coast** *(see pp30–31)*, beginning with breakfast on the Broadwalk in Hollywood Beach. Explore Dr. Von D. Mizell-Eula Johnson State Park before lunch in Fort Lauderdale.

AFTERNOON

Head up the coast to Palm Beach, touring the **Flagler Museum** *(see p30)*, **The Breakers** hotel *(see p30)*, and opulent **Worth Avenue** *(see p30)* before heading back to Miami.

Day ❸

MORNING

Stroll around **Downtown Miami** *(see pp90–97)*, then either take a boat tour of Biscayne Bay, or peruse exhibits at the **Pérez Art Museum** *(see p91)*. Head to **Little Havana** *(see pp18–19)* for lunch at **Versailles** *(see p97)*.

AFTERNOON

Head out to the **Everglades National Park** *(see pp34–5)* for the afternoon, getting a taster at Shark Valley, Mahogany Hammock, and the Anhinga and Gumbo Limbo trails.

Day ❹

MORNING

Get up early to drive Hwy-1 to **Key West** *(see pp32–3)*, stopping for a dip along the way at **Bahia Honda State Park** *(see p121)*, and perhaps a picnic.

AFTERNOON

Visit the **Hemingway Home** *(see p32)* and the **Mel Fisher Maritime Museum** *(see p122)* in Key West. Watch the sun set over **Mallory Square** *(see p32)*, and end the day with a "Duval Crawl" down **Duval Street** *(see p32)*.

Bahia Honda State Park has one of the best beaches in the world.

Top 10 Miami and the Keys Highlights

Art Deco apartments on Ocean Drive, lit up after sunset

Miami and the Keys Highlights	**10**
South Beach	**12**
Art Deco District	**14**
Calle Ocho, Little Havana	**18**
Vizcaya Museum and Gardens	**20**
Merrick's Coral Gables Fantasies	**24**
Lowe Art Museum	**26**
The Wolfsonian–FIU	**28**
Gold Coast	**30**
Key West	**32**
The Everglades	**34**

Miami and the Keys Highlights

There's much to love about Miami: tree-lined beaches, pastel-hued architecture, and a unique cultural scene. By day, the turquoise waters offer outdoor enthusiasts adventure aplenty, while historical sights abound for those so inclined. By night, the city's vibrant nightlife scene kicks into gear – it's party time.

1 South Beach

Ever since *Miami Vice* (see p83) drew attention to this fun-zone, visitors have flocked here for the beaches and nightlife (see pp12–13).

Art Deco District 2

The whimsical architecture on South Beach traces its roots back to 1920s Paris (see p17), but underwent a transformation and blossomed into Florida's own Tropical Deco (see pp14–15).

3 Calle Ocho, Little Havana

This street is still the heart of Cuban Miami, with local coffee shops, restaurants, and markets selling *cafecitos*, *batidos*, and tropical fruits (see pp18–19).

Vizcaya Museum and Gardens 4

Millionaire James Deering's aspiration to European grandeur and appreciation of decorative art led to the creation of Miami's most beautiful cultural treasure (see pp20–21).

5 Merrick's Coral Gables Fantasies

The 1920s boom saw a need to build not only structures but also a local identity. George Merrick rose to the challenge and created fantasy wonderlands that continue to stir the imagination today (see pp24–5).

0 km 5
0 miles 5

CAROL CITY
826
924
WESTVIEW
HIALEAH
GLADEVIEW
MIAMI SPRINGS
BROWNSVILLE
826
WEST MIAMI
Calle Ocho, Little Havana 3
Merrick's Coral Gables Fantasies
CORAL WAY VILLAGE
CORAL GABLES 4
5
Vizcaya Museum and Garden
6
Lowe Art Museum
874
SOUTH MIAMI
KENDALL
PINECREST

6 Lowe Art Museum

This renowned art museum showcases around 19,000 works of art, including masterpieces from all over the world, and from every age *(see pp26–7)*.

7 The Wolfsonian–FIU

Beginning life as a storage facility, this superb museum owes much to its founder's passion for collecting 20th-century propaganda art and design artifacts of the period 1885–1945 *(see pp28–9)*.

8 Gold Coast

Hugging the sands of the beautiful Gold Coast, Highway A1A wends its way through Florida's most iconic and beautiful areas *(see pp30–31)*.

9 Key West

A lively mix of maritime traditions and laid-back style, this sub-tropical island lives up to its reputation as a progressive, laid-back party town *(see pp32–3)*.

10 The Everglades

Taking up most of South Florida, the Everglades is a vast sea of swamp and sawgrass, dotted with subtropical forests and populated with an abundance of wildlife. It is also home to the Seminole and Miccosukee peoples *(see pp34–5)*.

TOP 10 ⭐ South Beach

SoBe, the nickname for Miami's beautiful South Beach, was inspired by Manhattan's SoHo, and it's become every bit as hip and fashionable as its New York counterpart. Now the "American Riviera" offers a mix of beach life, club-crawling, and alternative chic, attracting devotees from around the globe. Yet, SoBe's chic modern character blends pleasantly with just the right amount of light-hearted kitsch.

1 Lincoln Road Mall

Built by developer Carl Fisher in 1912, the Lincoln Road Mall **(below)** became a pedestrian mall in the 1960s. This fashionable area is lined with restaurants, shops, and galleries.

3 Lifeguard Huts

After a hurricane in 1992 destroyed most of the lifeguard stations, several artists were called in to create fun replacements. The best of these stands **(right)** can be found between 10th and 16th streets.

2 Villa Casa Casuarina

A Mediterranean Revival-style building, the Villa houses a hotel and a restaurant called Gianni's, which serves Italian food. Designer Gianni Versace once lived in the mansion.

4 Big Pink

This all-pink retro diner *(see p86)* is a SoBe mainstay. Browse through the morning paper over a full breakfast, or try the special "Big Pink TV Dinner", served on a steel tray.

NEED TO KNOW
MAP S6

Villa Casa Casuarina: restaurant open 11am–3:30pm & 5:30–10:30pm daily; www.vmmiami beach.com

O Cinema South Beach: www.o-cinema.org

■ Parking is a problem in the area, so once you find a place, leave the car and walk. Use the "Miami Beach Parking App" to identify municipal parking facilities, and pay via ParkMobile *(www. parkmobile.io)*. There are meters as well that accept credit cards (or cash).

■ To participate fully in the SoBe experience, the Big Pink *(see p86)* is the ideal place to grab a bite to eat or to catch-up on some reading.

Map of South Beach

7 Old City Hall

The buff-colored 1920s Mediterranean Revival tower **(left)** is a distinctive SoBe landmark. Its red-tile roof can be seen for blocks around. The building now houses the O Cinema South Beach movie theater.

LGBTQ+ RENAISSANCE

South Beach is a top destination for LGBTQ+ travelers. The LGBTQ+ scene took off here in the late 1980s and 1990s; the LGBTQ+ Visitor Center opened in 2010, and Miami Beach Gay Pride Parade debuted in 2012. Rainbow flags dotted throughout indicate gay-friendly businesses. The festivals, all-night events, and beach parties attract thousands from around the world. Many hotels offer packages geared toward LGBTQ+ guests.

9 SoBe Clubs

Most of South Beach's top clubs are located on Washington and Collins avenues, between 5th and 24th streets. Few get going until midnight at the earliest, but before long the party well and truly starts (see pp86–7).

10 Ocean Drive

Strolling, skating, or biking along this beachfront strip is the way the locals do it. Take in the bright tropical sun, the abundant, candy-colored Art Deco architecture (see pp14–17), and the many people-watching cafés.

5 Collins and Washington Avenues

These cool cousins of Ocean Drive offer quirky shops and fine Art Deco buildings, including the Miami Beach Post Office.

8 Lummus Park Beach

Much of the sand at this swath of busy park and 300-ft (90-m) wide beach **(below)** was imported. It stretches for ten blocks from 5th St north.

6 Española Way

This Mediterranean Revival enclave is all salmon-colored stucco, stripy awnings, and red-tile roofs. Built in 1922–5, it was meant to be an artists' colony but soon became a red-light district. It now houses boutiques and offbeat art galleries.

TOP 10 ⭐ Art Deco District

The Art Deco District of South Beach consists of more than 800 beautifully preserved buildings, the finest of them along Ocean Drive. This splendid array of structures embodies Miami's unique interpretation of the Art Deco style, which took the world by storm in the 1920s and 1930s. Florida's take on it is often called Tropical Deco, which befits the fun-and-sun approach to life. Often hotels were designed to look like ocean liners (Nautical Moderne) or styled with curving, streamlined features (Streamline Moderne).

Colony Hotel (1)
Perhaps the most famous of the Deco hotels along here, primarily because its blue neon sign **(right)**, has featured in so many movies and TV series.

(2) Beacon Hotel
The abstract decoration above the ground floor of the hotel has been brightened by a contemporary color scheme, an example of "Deco Dazzle," introduced by designer Leonard Horowitz in the 1980s.

(3) Breakwater Hotel
This Streamline Moderne hotel **(below)** was built in 1939. It features blue and white racing stripes and a striking central tower that recalls a ship's funnel. The tower lights up neon blue at night.

(4) Gabriel Hotel
Designed by famed architect Henry Hohauser in 1937, the former Celino Hotel transformed into the Gabriel in 2021, but retains its Nautical Deco theme.

(5) Waldorf Towers
Here stands one of the first examples (1937) of Nautical Moderne, where the style is carried to one of its logical extremes with the famous ornamental lighthouse on the hotel's roof. Fantasy towers were the stock-in-trade for Deco architects.

(6) Cardozo Hotel
A late Hohauser work (1939) and the favorite of Barbara Baer Capitman *(see p17)*, this is a Streamline masterpiece, in which the detail of traditional Art Deco is replaced with beautifully rounded sides, aerodynamic racing stripes, and other expressions of the modern age. The terrazzo floor utilizes this cheap version of marble to stylish effect. The hotel was reopened in 1982 and is now owned by the Cuban American singer Gloria Estefan.

7 Cavalier Hotel
A traditional Art Deco hotel **(left)**, which provides a contrast to the later Cardozo next door. Where the Cardozo emphasizes the horizontal and vaguely nautical, this facade is starkly vertical and temple-like. The temple theme is enhanced by beautifully ornate vertical stucco friezes, which recall the abstract, serpentine geometric designs of the Aztecs and other Meso-American cultures.

8 The Tides
An Art Deco masterpiece, the Tides resembles a luxury ocean liner. Completed in 1936, it was designed by the architect Lawrence Murray Dixon – a big name in the Art Deco history of South Beach. At 161 ft (49 m), it was briefly the tallest building in Miami.

9 Essex House
Hohauser's Essex House **(below)** is considered one of the best examples of maritime Art Deco architecture. Erected in 1938, the stark, white building closely resembles a ship, with "porthole" windows and awnings that look like railings. It isn't difficult to find this landmark; just look for the neon-lit spire.

Map of the Art Deco District

10 Leslie Hotel
The Leslie (1937) is white and yellow with gray accents **(above)** – a color scheme much in favor along Ocean Drive. Originally, however, Deco coloring was quite plain, usually white with only the trim in colors. Inside are shades of turquoise and flamingo pink.

Tropical Deco Features

Neon lights creating a blaze of color after sundown on Ocean Drive

 Neon
Used mostly for outlining architectural elements, neon lighting, in a range of colors, came into its own with Tropical Deco.

2 Ice-Cream Colors
Most Deco buildings here were originally white, with a bit of painted trim; the present-day rich pastel palette "Deco Dazzle" was the innovation of Miami designer and Capitman collaborator Leonard Horowitz in the 1980s.

3 Nautical Features
There's no better way to remind visitors of the ocean and its pleasures than with portholes and ship railings. Some of the buildings resemble beached liners.

 Curves and Lines
The suggestion of speed is the core of the Streamline Moderne style – it is an implicit appreciation of the power of technology.

5 Tropical Motifs
These motifs include Florida palms, panthers, orchids, and alligators, but especially birds, such as flamingos and cranes.

6 Stylized, Geometric Patterning
This was a nod to the extreme modernity of Cubism, as well as the power and precision of technology, espoused by Bauhaus precepts.

7 Stucco Bas-Relief Friezes
These sculptural bands provided Art Deco designers with

Stucco frieze, Cavalier Hotel
endless possibilities for a wonderful mix of ancient and modern motifs and themes for the buildings.

 Fantasy Towers
Many Art Deco buildings try to give the viewer a sense of something mythical – towers that speak of far shores or exalted visions – and that effectively announce the hotel's name, as well.

 Chrome
Nothing says "modern" quite like a cool and incorruptible silver streak of chrome. This material is used as detailing on and within many Deco buildings.

 Glass Blocks
Used in the construction of many Deco walls, the glass blocks give a sense of lightness in a part of the country where indoor-outdoor living is a year-round lifestyle.

THE STORY OF TROPICAL DECO

The Art Deco style took the world stage following the 1925 International Exhibition in Paris, synthesizing all sorts of influences, from Art Nouveau's flowery forms and Bauhaus to Egyptian imagery and the geometric patterns of Cubism. In 1930s America, Art Deco buildings reflected the belief that technology was the way forward, absorbing the speed and edginess of the Machine Age as well as the fantasies of science fiction and even a tinge of ancient mysticism. The thrilling new style was just what was needed to counteract the gloom of the Great Depression and give Americans a coherent vision for the future. In Miami, the style was exuberantly embraced and embellished upon with the addition of numerous local motifs, becoming "Tropical Deco." Its initial glory days were not to last long, however. Many hotels became soldiers' barracks in World War II and were torn down afterward. Fortunately, Barbara Baer Capitman *(see p39)* fought a famous battle to preserve these buildings. The Miami Beach Historic District was designated in 1979.

Example of Streamline Moderne style

TOP 10 ARCHITECTS

1 Henry Hohauser: Gabriel Hotel, Colony, Edison, Cardozo, Governor, Essex, Webster, Century, Taft

2 Albert Anis: Clevelander, Waldorf, Avalon, Majestic, Abbey, Berkeley Shore

3 Anton Skislewicz: Breakwater, Kenmore

4 L. Murray Dixon: Tiffany, Palmer House, Fairwind, Tudor, Senator, St. Moritz

5 Igor B. Polevitsky: Shelborne

6 Roy F. France: Cavalier

7 Robert Swartburg: Delano, The Marseilles

8 Kichnell & Elliot: Carlyle

9 Henry O. Nelson: Beacon

10 Russell Pancoast: The Bass

The bright pastel colors of the "Deco Dazzle" style, the creation of Leonard Horowitz, is perfectly portrayed in the Hotel Avalon building.

TOP 10 ⭐ Calle Ocho, Little Havana

Little Havana has been the heart of the Cuban community since Cubans first started settling here in the 1960s. Don't expect much in the way of sights – your time here is best spent soaking up the atmosphere. The area's heart is Southwest 8th Street, better known by its Spanish name, Calle Ocho. Its liveliest stretch, between SW 11th and SW 17th avenues, can be enjoyed on foot, but other points of interest can be reached by public bus, trolley, or ride share.

1 Plaza de la Cubanidad
At the plaza is a bronze map of Cuba (above) and an enigmatic quote by Cuban revolutionary hero José Martí.

2 Cuban Memorial Boulevard Park
The eternal flame of the Brigade 2506 Memorial honors the Cuban Americans who died in the Bay of Pigs invasion of Cuba in 1961. Other memorials pay tribute to Cuban heroes Antonio Maceo and José Martí, who fought against Spanish colonialism in the 1800s.

3 Domino Park
Cubans have gathered at the corner of SW 15th Ave (above) to match wits over games of dominoes for decades, making it an important meeting place.

4 Little Havana Visitors Center
If you're looking for Cuban souvenirs, this is the store for you (see p96). Shop for cigars, art, and coffee, as you sample the homemade ice cream.

NEED TO KNOW

MAP K3

Little Havana Cigar Factory: 1501 SW 8th St; 305 541 1103; open 10am–7pm Mon–Sat (to 6pm Sun); www.little havanacigars.com

■ You will have an easier time in this district if you can speak a good bit of Spanish, especially in shops or when phoning establishments.

■ Make sure you try the Cuban sampler platter at Versailles, with sweet plantains, cassava, and a Cuban tamale.

6 Calle Ocho Walk of Fame

Imitating Hollywood, pink marble stars embedded in the sidewalks **(left)** recognize not only Cuban celebrities, beginning with salsa singer Celia Cruz in 1987, but all famous Latin Americans with ties to South Florida.

LITTLE HAVANA: AN AMERICAN STORY

Named a National Treasure in 2017, this is Miami's most iconic neighborhood and, over time, has become a symbol of America's rich immigrant history. Political exiles, fleeing the turmoil and violence caused by the Cuban revolution, flocked here in thousands during the 1960s, creating this colorful enclave – one of the most vibrant in the city.

10 Cubaocho Museum and Performing Arts Center

This hybrid space *(see p93)* is both a rum cocktail bar, with live music, and a museum that celebrates Cuban culture with its exhibitions and events.

Map of Calle Ocho, Little Havana

A restaurant in the heart of Little Havana

5 José Martí Park

Named after a poet and patriot, this lush, tranquil oasis was dedicated in 1985 to the Cuban struggle for freedom. The site became a Tent City for the many homeless Mariel boatlift refugees in 1980.

7 Versailles

A trip to Miami is not complete without at least a snack at this legendary institution *(see p97)*. Versailles is a Cuban version of a fancy diner, with mirrors installed everywhere and a constant hubbub.

8 Woodlawn Park North Cemetery

Here lie the remains of two former Cuban presidents, including Gerardo Machado, as well as Nicaraguan dictator Anastasio Somoza.

9 Little Havana Cigar Factory

An inviting store and lounge **(left)** with decor inspired by 1950s cigar clubs.

TOP 10 ⭐ Vizcaya Museum and Gardens

Excessively opulent it may be, but the Vizcaya Museum is undeniably grand. It has the feel of a Renaissance-style villa, exactly what its makers – industrial magnate James Deering, designer Paul Chalfin, and architect F. Burrall Hoffman – intended when they built it in the early 1900s. Embodying a range of styles, both the genuine and ersatz have been skillfully assembled to evoke another culture, another continent, and another age.

1 Formal Gardens
The villa's elaborate formal gardens, extending over 10 acres (4 ha), are a highlight of the site. The splashing fountains of gracefully carved stone, statuary (**above**), and cleverly laid-out formal plantings offer myriad harmonious and ever-changing vistas. The evocative Secret Garden and playful Maze Garden conceal great artistry.

2 East Loggia
This portico frames magnificent views out over the sea and of the quaint stone breakwater known as the Barge. Carved in the shape of a large ship, it provides a perfect foreground to Key Biscayne, which lies just off the coast.

3 Italian Renaissance Dining Room
Another echo of the antique Italian taste, with a 2,000-year-old Roman table, a pair of 16th-century tapestries, and a full set of 17th-century chairs.

4 Italian Renaissance Living Room
Being the largest room in the house, the living room includes many notable pieces, such as a 2,000-year-old marble Roman tripod, a tapestry depicting the *Labors of Hercules*, a 15th-century Hispano-Moresque rug, and a Neapolitan altar screen.

5 Neo-Classical Entrance Hall and Library
The mood in these English Neo-Classical-style rooms (**right**) is more somber than other parts of the house. They were inspired by the work of Robert Adam.

6 Empire Bathroom
Few bathrooms in the world are more ornate than this marble, silver, and gilded affair. The bathtub was designed by Deering to run either fresh- or saltwater from the Biscayne Bay.

DEERING'S DREAM

Money was no object for industrialist James Deering. He wanted his winter residence to provide a sense of family history as well as luxury. Thus he bought and shipped bits of European pomp and reassembled them on this ideal spot right by the sea.

7 Rococo Music Room

All flowers and fluff, the music room **(above)** is graced with an exquisite Italian harpsichord dating from 1619, a dulcimer, and a harp.

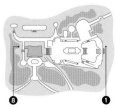

Key to Floor Plan
- Museum

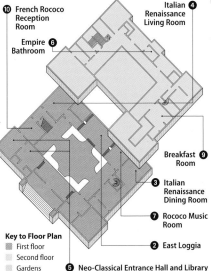

10 French Rococo Reception Room

4 Italian Renaissance Living Room

6 Empire Bathroom

9 Breakfast Room

3 Italian Renaissance Dining Room

7 Rococo Music Room

2 East Loggia

5 Neo-Classical Entrance Hall and Library

8 • **1**

Key to Floor Plan
- First floor
- Second floor
- Gardens

Floor Plan of the Vizcaya Museum and Gardens

9 Breakfast Room

On the upper floor, four ceramic Chinese Foo dogs guard the steps that ascend to the most bombastic room in the house.

10 French Rococo Reception Room

The assemblage is a mix of styles, but the look is of a salon under the 18th-century French King Louis XV. The tinted-plaster ceiling is from a Venetian palace.

8 Swimming Pool

This swimming pool extends under the house. Its walls are decorated with sea shells and depictions of marine life, and there are frescoes on the ceiling. The design is reminiscent of Italian homes on the canals of Venice.

NEED TO KNOW

MAP L6 ■ 3251 South Miami Ave ■ 305 250 9133 ■ www.vizcaya.org

Open 9:30am–4:30pm Wed–Mon (closed Thanksgiving and Christmas Day)

Adm $25; children $10; under-5s free

■ Take the guided tour to learn about Deering, as well as various legends, superstitions and quirks about many of the furnishings.

■ Enjoy Floridian food and exquisite wines at the on-site café. The museum's shop stocks delightful gift items.

Following pages Vizcaya Museum and Gardens

TOP 10 ★ Merrick's Coral Gables Fantasies

Coral Gables is a separate city within Greater Miami. Aptly described as the City Beautiful, its swanky homes line avenues shaded by giant banyans and oak trees, alongside canals. Regulations ensure that new buildings use the same architectural vocabulary advocated by George Merrick when he planned the city in the 1920s. He created an undeniable wonderland of a place that has not lost its aesthetic impact.

1 The Biltmore

George Merrick's 1926 masterpiece **(right)** has been refurbished and burnished to its original splendor and remains one of the most stunning hotels *(see p148)* in the country. It served as a military hospital during World War II and was a veteran's hospital until 1968. The 315-ft (96-m) near-replica of Seville's Giralda Tower is a local landmark.

2 French Normandy Village

The most homogeneous of all the villages at Coral Gables, this is all open timberwork, white stucco, and shake (cedar) roofs. Little alcoves and gardens here and there complete the picture-postcard look.

3 Venetian Pool

The claim that this is one of the most beautiful swimming pools **(below)** in the world is a fair one. Incorporating grottos and waterfalls, it was fashioned from a coral rock quarry in 1923 by Merrick's associates, Phineas Paist and Denman Fink *(see p107)*.

Map of Merrick's Coral Gables

4 French Country Village

Seven mansions are built in various styles typical of the French countryside. Some have open timber, stone, red brick, and shake (cedar) roofs, while others resemble the classic grange.

5 Chinese Village

An entire block has been transformed into a walled Chinese enclave. The curved, glazed-tile roofs are painted in vibrant colors, such as red and yellow. Some also feature motifs of dragons and bamboo.

6 Dutch South African Village

This collection of homes **(right)** embodies the high-peaked facades and scrolls of typical Dutch architecture, along with white stucco walls and red roofs associated with the Mediterranean. The style evolved as Dutch settlers adapted to African climes.

7 French City Village

Here you'll find nine *petits palais* in the French style, looking as if a city block of Paris has been airlifted to the US. The most elaborate confection is on the northwest corner of Cellini and Hardee.

8 Florida Pioneer Village

These are imitations of the early plantation and colonial homes built by Florida's first aristocrats. The style incorporates Neo-Classical, columned porches with the stucco walls of tropical tradition.

10 Italian Village

The typical country type of Italian villa, with its red-tile roof and painted stucco walls can be found here. Many later constructions have carried on the theme, so the original Merrick creations are almost lost in the mix.

9 Congregational Church

Coral Gables' first church **(below)**, built by Merrick in Spanish Baroque style, is a replica of a church in Costa Rica.

MERRICK THE VISIONARY

Merrick's dream was to build an American Venice. The project was the biggest real estate venture of the 1920s, costing around $100 million. The hurricane of 1926 then the Wall Street crash of 1929 left his city incomplete and Merrick himself destitute, but what remains is proof of his imagination.

NEED TO KNOW

MAP G3

Venetian Pool: 2701 De Soto Blvd; 305 460 5306; open times vary seasonally; closed Dec–Feb & national hols

Congregational Church: 3010 De Soto Blvd; 305 448 7421; services 9am & 11am Sun

■ Driving in Coral Gables can be tricky. Many streets have two names, and the signs spelled out on stucco blocks at the ground level can be hard to read at night.

■ Sample the salads and soups at Books and Books *(265 Aragon Ave)*.

TOP 10 ⭐ Lowe Art Museum

One of Miami's premier art venues, the Lowe was founded in 1950, and built in 1950–52 thanks to a donation from philanthropists Joe and Emily Lowe. Around 19,500 pieces showcase many of the world's most important artistic traditions, including those of the Renaissance and Baroque eras. The permanent collection incorporates 5,000 years of human history and in 2008, the Palley Pavilion was opened to showcase more than 100 works of contemporary glass art.

7 Ancient American
The collection covers all eras and areas, from about 1500 BCE to the 16th century. A silver disk engraved with complex iconography from 14th-century Peru is a rare piece and the colorful wood figurine **(below)** from Columbia is notable.

1 Contemporary Glass and Studio Arts
This stunning $3.5 million glass collection **(above)** features works by Dale Chihuly, Richard Jolley, and William Carlson.

2 Asian
One of the museum's strongest collections, with superb Chinese ceramics, as well as bronze and jade pieces, and other ceramics from Neolithic times to the 20th century. There is also classic, folk, and tribal art from India.

3 Egyptian
This excellent collection includes Coptic textiles, and there is also a jewel-like portrait sarcophagus mask, intended to resemble the features of the deceased. There are some medieval manuscripts on display too.

4 Native American
A Seminole shoulder bag, beautifully embroidered using thousands of tiny, colored-glass trade beads, is the pride of this collection. Also on show are Najavo, Hopi, and Apache art forms, which include masks, textiles, pottery, basketry, and brightly painted wooden *kachina* dolls.

5 Latin American
Important holdings of 20th-century art by Hispanic artists include Fernando Botero of Colombia, Arnaldo Roche-Rabell of Puerto Rico, and Carlos Alfonzo, who was born in Cuba.

6 17th-Century to Contemporary European and American
Some extraordinary works from this collection on permanent display include *Americanoom* by Chryssa, *Le Neveu de Rameau* by Frank Stella, *Football Player* by Duane Hanson, *Modular Painting in Four Panels* by Roy Lichtenstein, *Portrait of Mrs Collins* by Thomas Gainsborough, and *Rex* by Deborah Butterfield.

⑧ Greco-Roman

Classical sculpture is represented by marble carvings, including a bust of a Roman matron. The 6th-century BCE black-figure krater depicting Artemis, Leto, and Apollo is noteworthy.

⑨ Renaissance and Baroque

The exquisite collection of mostly paintings includes works by Battista Dossi, Tintoretto, Jordaens, Lucas Cranach the Elder, and Palma Vecchio.

⑩ African

The 16th-century cast bronze ring of the Yoruba people, depicting ritual decapitation, a Nok terracotta figure, and an Elpe or Ngbe society emblem assemblage all have an undeniable potency **(above)**.

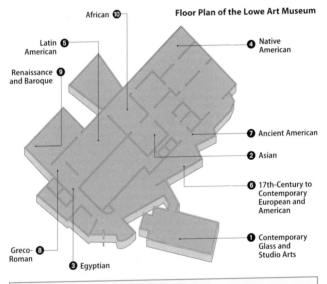

Floor Plan of the Lowe Art Museum

African ⑩

Latin ⑤
American

Renaissance ⑨
and Baroque

④ Native American

⑦ Ancient American

② Asian

⑥ 17th-Century to Contemporary European and American

① Contemporary Glass and Studio Arts

Greco- ⑧
Roman

③ Egyptian

NEED TO KNOW

MAP F3 ■ 1301 Stanford Dr ■ 305 284 2211 ■ www.lowe.miami.edu

Open 10am–4pm Wed–Sat

Adm free

■ Check out the museum store for a wide selection of beautifully illustrated books dedicated to the Lowe collection.

■ A local favorite, the **Titanic Brewing Company** *(5813 Ponce de Leon Blvd, 305 667 2537)* serves up seafood, live music, and hand-crafted ale.

Museum Guide

The Lowe is located in the middle of the campus of the University of Miami, which is located in southern Coral Gables and is easily accessible by the Miami Metrorail – just follow the signs. There is no particular order in which you are expected to visit the collections. Keep in mind that several of the galleries are always given over to special temporary exhibitions and events.

TOP 10 ⭐ The Wolfsonian–FIU

The building began life in the 1920s as the Washington Storage Company – Miami's wealthier winter residents used to store their valuables here when they were away. Eventually, in 1986, business-man Mitchell Wolfson, Jr. decided to buy it outright as a home for his vast assemblage of the rich detritus of modernity. The museum opened to the public in 1995 and houses around 200,000 objects, including decorative and propaganda art, furniture, and more.

1 Ceiling, Chandeliers, and Brackets
These unique decorative features **(above)** come from a 1920s Miami car showroom.

2 Art Deco Mailbox
To the left of the elevator is a wonder-ful 1929 Art Deco bronze mailbox, originally in New York Central Railroad Terminal, Buffalo.

3 The Wrestler
A symbol of The Wolfsonian–FIU **(left)**, this brawny, nude, life-sized form by American sculp-tor Dudley Talcott is made of aluminium, perhaps the classic metal of 20th-century modernity.

4 Harry Clarke Window
This literature-themed stained-glass window **(above)** was created in 1926–30 for the League of Nations' International Labor Organization in Geneva, Switzerland.

5 Entrance Hall

The massive ceiling supports reflect the Mediterranean Revival style of the facade and are original. So are the terracotta floors, the woodwork over the doors leading to the elevator vestibule, and the rough stucco walls. All of the ornamental cast stone was done by hand.

6 Bridge Tender's House

Standing just north of The Wolfsonian's entrance is this remarkable 1939 building, a stainless-steel hexagonal structure that has been designed in the Art Moderne style.

NEED TO KNOW

MAP R4 ▪ 1001 Washington Ave, Miami Beach ▪ 305 531 1001 ▪ www.wolfsonian.org

Open 10am–6pm Wed–Sun (to 9pm Fri); closed national hols

Adm $12; concessions $8; under-6s free

▪ Special social events are held on some evenings.

▪ Private tours can be arranged by appointment.

▪ The museum library and research center can be accessed by appointment only.

7 Fountain

Positioned under a skylight, the fountain **(left)** was made from an elaborate Deco window grille from the Norris Theater in Pennsylvania. Composed of over 200 gilded and glazed terracotta tiles, the richly floral decoration belies the careful geometrical structure of the piece.

8 Wooden Staircase

This fine piece of modern woodcraft is fashioned from pine and steel. It came from the Curtis Bok residence, Gulph Mills, Pennsylvania, designed by Wharton Esherick in 1935.

9 Temporary Exhibits

Much of the space is used for special exhibits exploring themes of the modern age. The Wolfsonian is a leading authority on propaganda art, showing how savvy designers have used the science of psychology to their advantage, to create highly persuasive images for businesses and governments.

ORIENTATION

The Wolfsonian–FIU is a museum and a design research institute. Three floors are offices and storage and are not normally open to the public. Your tour should begin outside, progress to the Entrance Hall, then up the back elevator to floors 5, 6, and 7.

Floor Plan of The Wolfsonian–FIU

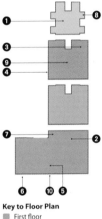

Key to Floor Plan
- ▪ First floor
- ▪ Fifth floor
- ▪ Sixth floor
- ▪ Seventh floor

10 Mediterranean Revival Building

The Spanish Baroque-style relief around the main entrance **(above)** is a striking feature. The bronze flagpoles and finials date from 1914.

TOP 10 ⭐ Gold Coast

The best way to get a feel for Florida's East Coast is to travel down the Gold Coast between West Palm Beach and Miami. The 50-mile (80-km) road hugs the beach, passing nature preserves, and historic, ocean view neighborhoods. Though an easy day trip, it's worth taking your time to enjoy art, gilded-age sights, and sunshine along the way. At a slower pace, much of this route can also be done on public transportation by taking the Brightline intercity train and local buses.

Flagler Museum

An iconic, historic landmark **(right)**, this mansion was Henry M. Flagler's *(see p39)* wedding gift to his third wife, Mary Lily Kenan, who was half his age and an heiress herself. The trappings of royalty are visible everywhere, right down to the mid-18th century Louis XV commode.

2 Norton Museum of Art

Perhaps Florida's finest museum of art *(see p43)*, featuring more than 8,200 Impressionist, Modern American, Chinese, and European works of art.

3 The Breakers

The aura of America's Gilded Age (1877–96) still clings to this stylish abode **(below)**, from the frescoed Italianate ceilings to the crystal chandeliers *(see p148)*. It is the third hotel to be built on this site, the first two having burned down.

4 Las Olas Boulevard, Fort Lauderdale

Fort Lauderdale's main street has upscale shops and restaurants. Las Olas Riverfront is a colorful mall, from which a river cruise departs.

5 Worth Avenue, Palm Beach

The street for local and visiting VIPs to select this week's wardrobe and perhaps a little *objet d'art*.

6 Dr. Von D. Mizell-Eula Johnson State Park

A long barrier island that commands views of busy Port Everglades as well as a beach historically significant as one designated for African Americans in the days of segregation. It is now a destination popular with the LGBTQ+ community *(see p62)*.

7 Bonnet House

Built in 1920, this period home (left) is full of the personality of its creators, Frederic and Evelyn Bartlett. They were both artists, as is evident from the highly original murals and the somewhat eccentric tropical gardens.

8 Gumbo Limbo Nature Center

An informative center, with a boardwalk that winds through mangroves and hammocks (raised areas) in Red Reef Park (see p55). It takes its name from the gumbo limbo tree, which has distinctive, red peeling bark.

9 Boca Raton Museum of Art

Located inside the beautiful Mizner Park in downtown Boca Raton, this art museum hosts world-class exhibitions. Its impressive permanent collection includes 19th-, 20th-, and 21st-century art, sculpture, and photography.

ALL THAT GLITTERS

Here, all that glitters is probably gold! The Gold Coast may be named for the gold doubloons that Spanish galleons used to transport along the intracoastal waterways, but these days the term is used more for the golden lifestyle of the many millionaires and billionaires who have winter homes here.

Map of the Gold Coast

NEED TO KNOW

Flagler Museum: **MAP D2**; 1 Whitehall Way, Palm Beach; www.flaglermuseum.us

Norton Museum of Art: **MAP D2**; 1450 S. Dixie Hwy, W Palm Beach; www.norton.org

Boca Raton Museum of Art: **MAP D3**; 501 Plaza Real, Boca Raton; www.boca museum.org

■ Take the three-hour Jungle Queen Cruise (www.junglequeen.com) to get the most out of Fort Lauderdale.

■ Have lunch in Fort Lauderdale at Noodles Panini (821 East Las Olas Blvd, www.noodlespanini.com). At dinnertime, head for Bistro Mezzaluna (1821 SE 10th Ave, www.bistromezzaluna.com).

10 The Broadwalk

Lined with shops, bars, and restaurants – including the popular beach shack Riptide Tiki Bar – this is the famous stretch of Hollywood Beach (above). It runs for 2.5 miles (4 km) from Jefferson Street to Sheridan.

TOP 10 ★ Key West

Claimed by Spanish colonists in 1513, this tiny island or key, measuring approximately 4 miles (6.5 km) in length and just about 2 miles (3 km) in width, has changed in status from a pirates' den to one of the most prosperous cities per capita in the United States. Always attracting free-thinkers and eccentrics, Key West has a unique character that is still apparent despite the upscale tourism industry that has developed since the 1990s. The island's self-named Conch (pronounced "konk") inhabitants include many writers, artists, and New-Agers.

1 Custom House Museum
Located inside the imposing old Customs House **(above)**, this museum of art and history exhibits paintings of some of the island's eccentrics and notables, along with accounts of life here in various epochs.

2 Mallory Square
Every evening at sunset, the fun-loving citizens of the self-styled "Conch Republic" throw a party in this square, complete with entertainers.

3 Audubon House and Tropical Gardens
The house offers visitors a glimpse into mid-19th-century island life. The "ghosts" of the family who lived here take you on an audio tour through the impressive rooms.

4 Duval Street
The main street of Old Town **(above)** is the place to do the "Duval Crawl" – the arduous task of stopping in at all of the 100 or so bars, pubs, and clubs that line Duval Street and its environs.

5 The Hemingway Home
Ernest Hemingway lived from 1931 to 1940 in this Spanish colonial-style coral rock house **(right)**. Remnants of his stay include the supposed descendants of his six-toed cats.

6 Key West Cemetery
The tombs are raised to avoid flooding as the soil is mostly hard coral rock. Droll epitaphs include "I told you I was sick" on the tomb of a hypochondriac.

Map of Key West

7 Mel Fisher Maritime Museum

This engaging museum *(see p122)* is dedicated to the lure and romance of sunken treasure and the equipment that has been used to retrieve it. Most impressive are the gold artifacts retrieved from 17th-century Spanish galleons.

THE BUSINESS OF WRECKING

The coral reef that surrounds Key West has been responsible for many shipwrecks. In the 1700s, these waters were fished by Bahamians, who patrolled the reef to salvage shipwrecks for trade goods. This scavenging was known as "wrecking". It grew so popular that in 1825 an act of the US congress legislated for tighter control and decreed that only US residents could have salvage rights.

8 Fort Zachary Taylor Historic State Park

The 1866 brick fort is now a military museum with a fine collection of Civil War artifacts.

9 Bahama Village

An archway over Petronia Street **(above)** at Duval marks the entrance to this neighborhood, where the first Black Bahamian settlers arrived in the 19th century. Head to the Bahama Market and Blue Heaven restaurant for a slice of Island culture.

10 Lighthouse and Keeper's Quarters

Opened in 1848, Key West's lighthouse could beam light 25 miles (40 km) out to sea. Climb the 88 steps to enjoy panoramic seascapes and views of the town.

NEED TO KNOW

MAP A6

Visitor Information: Chamber of Commerce, 510 Greene St ▪ www. keywestchamber.org

Custom House Museum: open 10am–5pm daily; adm; www.kwahs.org

Audubon House and Tropical Gardens: open 9:30am–4:15pm daily; adm; https://audubon house.org

The Hemingway Home: open 9am–5pm daily; adm; www.hemingwayhome.com

Key West Cemetery: open sunrise–sunset daily

Mel Fisher Maritime Museum: open 10am–4pm daily; adm; www.melfisher.org

Fort Zachary Taylor Historic State Park: open 8am–sunset daily; adm; www.floridastateparks.org

Lighthouse and Keeper's Quarters: open 10am–4:30pm daily; adm

TOP 10 ★ The Everglades

Comprising one of the planet's most fascinating ecosystems, the Everglades is a vast, shallow river system of swamps and wetlands, where the waters can take a year or more to meander from the Kissimmee River, northwest of Miami, into Florida Bay. At least 45 plant varieties grow here that are found nowhere else on earth. It is also home to over 350 kinds of bird, 300 types of fish, and dozens of reptile and mammal species.

1 Big Cypress Swamp

This shallow wetland is a range of wet and dry habitats determined by slight differences in elevation. It is home to the Florida panther.

5 Royal Palm Visitor Center

Both Anhinga and Gumbo Limbo trails begin at the Royal Palm Visitor Center, the site of Florida's first state park **(right)**.

2 Corkscrew Swamp

 A boardwalk **(above)** leads through various habitats, including old cypress full of nesting birds. The threatened wood stork has been seen here.

3 Ah-Tah-Thi-Ki and Billie Swamp

The Ah-Tah-Thi-Ki Museum focuses on Seminole culture *(see p42)*. Billie Swamp has exhilarating airboat rides and informative Buggy Eco-Tours, from which you might spot alligators.

6 Mahogany Hammock

Near Flamingo is one of the park's largest hammocks (fertile mounds), where a trail meanders through dense tropical growth. This is home to colorful tree snails and the largest mahogany tree in the country.

7 Fakahatchee Strand

This is one of Florida's wildest areas **(below)**, a 20-mile (32-km) slough (muddy backwater), noted for its rare orchids, unique air plants, and the largest stand of native royal palms in the US. There are boardwalks and rangers on hand.

4 Shark Valley

This area, only 17 miles (27 km) from the western edge of Miami, has a 15-mile (24-km) loop road that you can travel by bicycle or on a narrated tram ride. It ends at a tower that affords great views.

⑧ Everglades National Park

The park features elevated boardwalks, tours, canoe rental **(above)**, camping, and accommodation.

PRESERVING THE EVERGLADES

The Everglades evolved over a period of more than six million years, but humans almost destroyed its fragile balance in less than 100. In the 1920s, the Hoover Dike closed off the area's main water source, Lake Okeechobee; Highway 41 further blocked its flow. Environmentalist Marjory Stoneman Douglas reversed the situation. Today, work continues slowly on building levees around the area to help keep the vital moisture in.

⑩ Flamingo

This outpost was badly damaged by Hurricane Irma in September 2017. However, sportfishing, camping, and canoeing are possible. In 2023, the renovated Guy Bradley Visitor Center reopened along with a new lodge and restaurant.

Map of the Everglades

⑨ Tamiami Trail (US 41)

This was the first road to open up the area by linking the Atlantic and Gulf coasts. It passes pioneer camps, such as Everglades City and Chokoloskee, which have barely changed since the late 1800s. They mark the western entrance to Everglades National Park.

NEED TO KNOW

MAP C4

Big Cypress Swamp: Oasis Visitor Center; 239 695 4111

Corkscrew Swamp: 375 Sanctuary Rd; https://corkscrew.audubon.org

Ah-Tah-Thi-Ki Museum: 34725 W Boundary Rd, Clewiston; www.ahtah thiki.com

Billie Swamp: www.billieswamp.com

Shark Valley: 305 221 8776 (visitor center)

Royal Palm Visitor Center: 305 242 7700

Fakahatchee Strand: 239 961 1925

Everglades National Park: 305 242 7700; www.nps.gov/ever

Flamingo: 239 695 2945 (visitor center)

■ **Visit early, when many animals are active. Keep to the boardwalks.**

The Top 10
of Everything

Historic Sites
  and Monuments   **38**

Architectural Wonders   **40**

Museums   **42**

Romantic Spots   **44**

**Diving by the submerged Christ
of the Abyss statue, off Key Largo**

Spots for People-Watching	**46**	Nightlife	**64**
Parks and Gardens	**48**	Restaurants	**66**
Beaches	**50**	Chic Shopping Centers	**68**
Sports and Outdoor Activities	**52**	Malls and Markets	**70**
Snorkeling and Diving	**54**	Miami and the Keys for Free	**72**
Off the Beaten Path	**56**	Festivals	**74**
Children's Attractions	**58**	Walks, Drives, and Cycling Routes	**76**
Performing Arts Venues	**60**		
LGBTQ+ Venues	**62**		

Historic Sites and Monuments

Coral Castle, a mysterious sculpture created by Edward Leedskalnin

1 Vizcaya Museum and Gardens

James Deering's opulent monument with its rich artistic traditions has become Miami's most beloved social and cultural center *(see pp20–21)*.

2 Ancient Spanish Monastery

Built in 1133–41 in Segovia, Spain, this monastic building *(see p99)* was bought by William Randolph Hearst in 1925 and shipped to New York. The parts were reassembled here in 1952.

3 Charles Deering Estate

James Deering's half-brother built this residence *(see p116)* for himself. The original 19th-century house, Richmond Cottage, was restored after being damaged by Hurricane Andrew in 1992.

4 Coral Gables Merrick House

This is the house *(see p111)* where the Merrick family lived in the early 1900s and where master builder, George Merrick, grew up. The contrast between the modest surroundings of his home and the spectacle of his grandiose dreams is fascinating.

5 Coral Castle

This monument *(see p115)* to unrequited love speaks volumes about early Florida's place in US history as a refuge for misfits, eccentrics, and visionaries. Land was cheap (the creator of Coral Castle bought his acre plot for $12 in 1920) and the population was sparse, so it was easy to do your own thing without being bothered. But how this gargantuan folly was actually constructed remains an enigma.

6 Brigade 2506 Memorial

Little Havana's Eternal Flame and monument garden *(see p18)* remembers those who died in the Bay of Pigs debacle, attempting to reclaim Cuba from Fidel Castro's regime in 1961.

7 Holocaust Memorial

MAP R2 ▪ 1933–45 Meridian Ave, South Beach ▪ 305 538 1663 ▪ www.holocaust memorialmiamibeach.org

Miami has one of the largest populations of Holocaust survivors in the world, so this stunning monument

Bronze Holocaust Memorial

has extra poignancy. Sculpted by Kenneth Treister and finished in 1990, the centerpiece is a huge bronze forearm bearing a stamped number from Auschwitz. The arm is thronged with nearly 100 life-sized figures in positions of suffering. The surrounding plaza has a graphic pictorial history of the Holocaust, and a granite wall listing the names of thousands of concentration camp victims.

8 Indian Key Historic State Park

This Florida Keys island preserve *(see p122)* is rich in history. In the 1830s, a community of wreckers briefly thrived here before being destroyed in the Second Seminole War.

9 The Barnacle

Built in 1891, this is Dade County's oldest house *(see p108)*, which cleverly uses ship-building techniques to make it stormproof as well as comfortable, allowing for Florida's steamy climate.

House at Barnacle Historic State Park

10 Stranahan House

MAP D3 ▪ 335 SE 6th Ave, near Las Olas ▪ 954 524 4736 ▪ Adm

Fort Lauderdale's oldest house was built originally in 1901 as a trading post for the Seminoles. The handsome two-story riverside house is furnished with period antiques, but it is the photos that best evoke the past, such as Stranahan trading alligator hides, otter pelts, and egret plumes with the local Seminoles. Such prizes were brought in from the Everglades in dugout canoes.

TOP 10 MOVERS AND SHAKERS

Marjory Stoneman Douglas

1 Marjory Stoneman Douglas
The first of Florida's environmentalists, who single-handedly saved the Everglades from development. She died in 1998, at the age of 108.

2 Betty Mae Tiger Jumper
Became the first and only female chief of the Seminole Tribe of Florida in 1967. She also founded the tribe's newspaper.

3 Roxcy Bolton
Miami-based civil rights activist (1926–2017), with a focus on women's rights.

4 Manny Diaz
This Cuban American politician served as mayor of Miami from 2001 to 2009. He was credited with restoring the city's finances.

5 Ruth Bryan Owen
Florida's first female US Representative in Congress, and later the first woman appointed as a US ambassador.

6 The Deering Brothers
James *(see pp20–21)* and Charles *(see p116)* built homes that are now major attractions in Miami.

7 William Brickell
One of the first men to take advantage of the Homestead Act of 1862.

8 Barbara Baer Capitman
Capitman was the driving force behind the movement to save the area's Art Deco hotels *(see p17)*.

9 Julia Tuttle
The dynamic pioneer who convinced Henry Flagler to extend his railroad down to Miami, in 1896.

10 Chief Jim Billie
This controversial Seminole chief was responsible for bringing wealth to his tribe in the 1980s, by building casinos on reservations.

Architectural Wonders

1 Art Deco District

A national treasure of uplifting architecture (see pp14–17). In saving it, South Miami Beach not only transformed itself but also inspired a national movement to preserve historic structures.

2 Atlantis on Brickell

MAP M5 ▪ 2025 Brickell Ave

Built by Arquitectonica in 1982 and soon thereafter one of the stars of *Miami Vice*, this "building with the hole in it" is in danger of being overrun by the construction going on along Brickell. The "hole" is an ingenious 37-ft (11-m) cube cut out of the building's center, at the 12th floor. A red spiral staircase and a palm tree draw your attention to it in a delightful way.

3 The Biltmore and Coral Gables Congregational Church

Facing each other across gardens, these two structures (see pp24–5) are the heart of George Merrick's contribution to "the City Beautiful".

The iconic Biltmore, Coral Gables

Freedom Tower, a city landmark

4 Freedom Tower

A soaring edifice (see p90) inspired by the famous belfry of Seville's vast cathedral, La Giralda is home to Miami Dade College's Museum of Art and Design.

5 Fontainebleau Hotel

Designed by architect Morris Lapidus, this landmark (see p150) defines the Miami Modern Architecture (MiMo) style: sweeping lines, colors, and inlaid marble floors with the trademark bow-tie motif.

6 Ingraham Building

MAP N2 ▪ 25 SE 2nd Ave, at Flagler St, Downtown

This Renaissance-Revival beauty is an unmissable landmark, and it evokes all the glamour of the 1920s boom era.

7 Estefan Enterprises

MAP R5 ▪ 420 Jefferson Ave, Miami Beach

A playful building that takes the frivolity of Deco several steps further, with a free-form green-wave tower slicing through a cool blue cube, evoking both sea and sky.

8 1111 Lincoln Road
MAP Q2 ■ 1111 Lincoln Rd, at Alton Rd, South Beach

Dubbed "the most famous parking garage in the world," this unique open-air structure, completed in 2010 by Swiss architectural firm Herzog & de Meuron, looks like a precarious stack of cards.

9 Miami Tower
I. M. Pei's *(see p92)* striking take on the ziggurat theme, so often used in Art Deco, looks for all the world like a stepped stack of CDs in various sizes. It is especially appealing at night when lit up with vibrant colors.

The Miami Tower lit up at dusk

10 Key West Old Town
This small island *(see pp32–3)* has one of the US's largest collections of 19th-century structures. About 4,000 buildings, mostly houses, embody the distinctive local style. Many architectural features take their cues from elements used on ships, such as roof hatches to allow air circulation. A unique innovation is the "eyebrow" house, with second-floor windows hidden under a front porch roof overhang, providing shade in the heat.

TOP 10 MURALS AND MOSAICS

Stunning mosaic, Bacardi Building

1 Bacardi Building
2100 Biscayne Blvd
Don't miss the tropical foliage mosaic, and note the building next to it, too.

2 Ladies in White
Calle Ocho (SW 8th St) & 15th Av, Little Havana
This mural is created by local street artist Daniel Fila, also known as Krave Art.

3 The Good Wall
982 SW 8th S, Little Havana
Alley of murals that change regularly.

4 Miami Beach Post Office
1300 Washington Ave, South Beach
The classy Deco rotunda of the old post office has a triptych mural of Ponce de León and the Native American peoples.

5 Coral Gables City Hall
405 Biltmore Way
Denman Fink created the mural on the bell tower's interior. The one above the stairs is by John St. John.

6 Culmer Overtown Branch Library
350 NW 13th St
Local artist Purvis Young painted the "Everyday Life" mural here in 1984.

7 Welcome to Miami Beach
770 Arthur Godfrey Rd, Miami Beach
A postcard on the side of The Roosevelt Theatre painted by artist Lebo.

8 The Society of the Four Arts
Four Arts Plaza, Palm Beach
See allegorical murals from 1939.

9 Wyland Whaling Walls
201 William St, Key West
An undersea world of whales and other cetaceans is featured here.

10 Bahama Village
Thomas St at Petronia St
A charming mural evokes daily life in the Bahama Village neighborhood.

🔟 Museums

The vibrant bar at Cubaocho Museum

1 Cubaocho Museum

Learn more about Little Havana's history and culture at this small, yet informative, museum and art gallery (see p93). Cuban culture has been a key factor in Miami's identity since the 1950s, a legacy explored through revolving exhibits of Cuban art, an old-fashioned café, a bar serving stellar mojitos and live Cuban arts performances.

2 Jewish Museum of Florida

With its stained-glass windows and Deco details, the former synagogue itself is as fascinating as the exhibits it houses.

Modern design, The Wolfsonian–FIU

The museum (see p83) is dedicated to telling the story of the 230-year Jewish presence in Florida.

3 The Wolfsonian–FIU

The perfect complement to the Art Deco District, this museum and design research institute (see pp28–9) has a wealth of modern design exhibits.

4 Naomi Wilzig Erotic Art Museum

MAP R4 ■ Mezzanine level 1205 Washington Ave ■ 305 532 9336 ■ Open 11am–6pm daily ■ Adm ■ www.weammuseum.com

An extensive collection of erotic art from around the world, valued at a whopping $10 million.

5 Ah-Tah-Thi-Ki Seminole Indian Museum

This excellent museum (see p34), on the Big Cypress Indian Reservation, features Seminole artifacts, such as pottery and beautiful clothing. The Green Corn Ceremony is also explained, including the games, music, dance, and costumes involved. A nature trail leads through the cypress canopy, where signs explain the use of certain flora in Seminole culture.

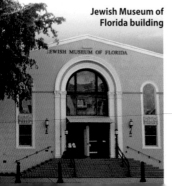

Jewish Museum of Florida building

JEWISH MUSEUM OF FLORIDA

6 Mel Fisher Maritime Museum

Immerse yourself in the romance of long-lost, booty-laden shipwrecks at this fascinating museum (see p122).

7 HistoryMiami Museum

MAP M2 ■ 101 W Flagler St ■ 305 375 1492 ■ Open 10am–4pm Wed–Sat (from noon Sun) ■ Adm ■ www.historymiami.org

Starting as far back in prehistory as 12,000 years, the museum slips swiftly through the millennia to reach Spanish colonization, Seminole culture, extravagance in the "Roaring Twenties," and Cuban immigration in more recent years.

8 Lowe Art Museum

This is one of Miami's top art museums (see pp26–7), featuring works from European, American, Chinese, Pre-Columbian, and Native American cultures.

9 Norton Museum of Art

One of South Florida's finest museums (see p30). Its collection displays works by Europeans, such as Rembrandt, Goya, Renoir, and Picasso, and Americans including O'Keeffe and Pollock. The museum also has photography and contemporary art.

Entrance to Pérez Art Museum Miami

10 Pérez Art Museum Miami

Besides impressive temporary shows, the museum's permanent collection (see p91) focuses on art since the 1940s, and includes artistic works by Frankenthaler, Gottlieb, Rauschenberg, and Stella. It's set in lovely gardens.

TOP 10 CONTEMPORARY COLLECTIONS

Wynwood Walls graffiti

1 Wynwood Walls
2520 NW 2nd Ave
A cutting-edge project brings the world's greatest graffiti artists to Miami.

2 Margulies Collection
591 NW 27th St
Important photography collection, plus sculpture, video, and large installations.

3 Nina Johnson
6315 NW 2nd Ave
A gallery of one of Miami's top dealers featuring emerging and known artists.

4 Institute of Contemporary Art (ICA)
61 NE 41st St
Displays works by emerging artists as well as internationally renowned masters of contemporary art.

5 Bernice Steinbaum Gallery
2101 Tigertail Ave
Steinbaum moved her groundbreaking art gallery from NYC to Miami in the year 2000.

6 Artspace/Virginia Miller Galleries
169 Madeira Ave, Coral Gables
Historically significant Latin American art, including paintings and photography.

7 Locust Projects
297 NE 67th St
Specializing in artistic innovations and experimental new art.

8 Rubell Museum
1100 NW 23rd St
About 1,000 works by modern artists, including Haring, Koons, Basquiat, and Cuban artist José Bedia.

9 Cernuda Arte
3155 Ponce de Leon Blvd, Coral Gables
Cuban art from all periods.

10 Fredric Snitzer Gallery
1540 NE Miami Ct
Features Latin American and avant-garde Cuban contemporary art.

🔟 Romantic Spots

Gardens adorned with water features of carved stone, Vizcaya Museum

1 Vizcaya Museum and Gardens

This is a glorious pastiche of styles from more or less 500 years of European architecture. Most of it was bought by an early-20th-century farm machinery magnate to be remodeled into this comfortable palace, surrounded by enchanting gardens (see pp20–21).

2 Coral Castle

One lovesick Latvian immigrant, Edward Leedskalnin, created this huge coral rock Valentine heart (see p115) to win back his fickle love. The

woman remained unmoved by his Herculean labors, however, and he died here alone in 1951.

3 Fairchild Tropical Botanic Garden

The tranquil, silvery lakes, fragrant, shaded bowers, and lush, dappled retreats are capable of bringing out the romantic in anyone. Explore at your own pace, or take it all in with the 40-minute tram tour – before dinner at the nearby Redfish by Chef Adrianne (see p119).

4 Ancient Spanish Monastery Cloister and Gardens

With its magnificent gardens and cloisters redolent of ancient lands and courtly love, this has become a popular spot for weddings. The building (see p99) can be traced back to 12th-century Spain, though it didn't make its way to Florida until the 20th-century. Having lain dormant in packing crates for years, it was finally reassembled in the 1950s.

5 Venetian Pool

A lush fantasy of sculpted stone, water, and gardens, where Esther Williams (American competitive swimmer and actress) used to star in synchronized swimming movies. The pool (see p24) was born of the mind of entrepreneur George Merrick.

6 Morikami Japanese Gardens

The 1,000-year-old originals of some of these deeply peaceful settings were designed for Japanese nobility – places of inspiration for them to recite poetry to each other, or to seek solace in troubled times. Few places evoke the serenity and spiritual depth you can sense here (see p45), in the silent rocks and the murmuring cascades.

7 Hotel St. Michel

French-style boutique hotel (see p151) with an exquisite restaurant. Stay a night or two and you'll think you're in a chic little pension in Paris. The subtly lit bistro is a perfect place for a quietly intimate tête-à-tête, yet all this is within walking distance of downtown Coral Gables.

8 Cape Florida Light

MAP H4 ■ 1200 S Crandon Blvd, Key Biscayne ■ 305 361 8779 ■ Open for tours at 10am & 1pm Thu–Mon ■ www.floridastateparks.org/park/Cape-Florida

Bill Baggs Cape Florida State Park contains this historic lighthouse

Cape Florida Light

(see p93), which was built in 1825 and soars 95 ft (30 m) into the sky. As the surrounding beaches and scrub are completely untouched, climbing the 109 steps affords mesmerizing views; it's a popular spot for loved-up couples who come here to propose.

Watching the sunset, Mallory Square

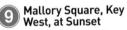

9 Mallory Square, Key West, at Sunset

Although you will most likely be there (see p32) with a hoard of other sunset-viewers, the beauty of this moment and the general air of merriment will provide you with a memorable experience. Watch tall ships sail in front of the huge setting sun, blazing orangy-pink at the Gulf's edge. True romantics should keep an eye out for the beguiling green flash that's said to occur just before the sun disappears below the horizon – if you catch it, it means good luck in love.

10 NOMA Beach at Redfish

Perhaps the most starry-eyed setting in Miami, the former Redfish Grill reopened in 2022 with celebrity chef Donatella Arpaia at the helm (see p119). It retained the shimmering bay views, romantic lighting, and backdrop of nearby saltwater Atoll Pool. The menu now focuses on coastal Italian dishes, with fresh seafood and pasta.

🔟 Spots for People-Watching

A late-night gathering at Clevelander

 Clevelander
This hotel's *(see p88)* beachfront cafés evolve into one of SoBe's top pool-bar scenes after dark. Its proximity to the beach inspires a casual style, and there's always a crowd to enjoy happy hour and live music.

② **Ocean Drive**
The epitome of the "American Riviera" *(see p13)*. Sit in a café, or cruise in a convertible, on skates, or simply on foot. Sizzling with energy, Ocean Drive is a catwalk for a constant procession of avant-garde fashion.

③ **Bayside Marketplace**
There is never a dull moment in Downtown Miami's hottest daytime spot *(see p92)*, which features a variety of boutiques, live music, street performers, and dining right on the marina.

④ **Lincoln Road Mall**
Second only to Ocean Drive in its star-quality appeal. Lined with sculpture-fountains and plants, this pedestrian area with its outdoor food spots *(see p82)* is always lively.

⑤ **Big Pink**
This busy, retro diner *(see p86)* welcomes its customers with a charming, signature pink Volkswagen Beetle that stands outside. Open all night, the diner is known for its breakfast and its "Big Pink TV Dinner".

⑥ **Joe's Stone Crab**
Established in 1913, this cozy family restaurant and crab shack has grown to become one of Miami's legendary institutions and a perennial favorite with many celebrities *(see p89)*. The Florida stone crab, served in its shell with mustard sauce, is a classic. The

Famous Art Deco architecture along fashionable Ocean Drive

restaurant also serves timeless dishes, such as fried chicken, hashed browns, and key lime pie.

7 Commodore Plaza

Coconut Grove's second most frequented spot is this intersection, where every corner features a top viewing position for the constant circulation of pedestrian traffic, everyone scoping out a café or restaurant, and each other. Try the GreenStreet Café *(see p110)*.

8 Hollywood Broadwalk

The Broadwalk *(see p31)* is a rare swath of beach where a 2.5-mile (4-km) pedestrian walkway fronts directly on to the sand, just to the north of Miami Beach. It's non-stop surfside fun, with loads of revelers of all kinds cruising up and down.

Popular at sunset, Mallory Square

9 Mallory Square, Key West

At sunset, this huge Key West square *(see p32)* at the Gulf end of Duval Street is a gathering place for all kinds of locals and visitors. Street performers keep it lively, and there are many vendors of food and souvenirs.

10 CocoWalk

A host of high-end dining experiences, chic outdoor cafés, shops, and a cineplex provide entertainment. But, here *(see p107)* in the heart of the Grove, it's great just to stroll along the lush, tree-lined streetscape and hang out in the central, open-air courtyard.

TOP 10 TRENDY CAFÉS

Charming exterior of Pepes Café

1 Pepes Café
An old-school diner since 1909, this place serves up big breakfast plates, steaks, and Key West's conchs.

2 Eternity Coffee Roasters
The best coffee shop in Downtown Miami, roasting Colombian coffee beans in-house.

3 GreenStreet Café
Coconut Grove's numero uno for people-watching, happy hour, and creative meals *(see p110)*.

4 Berries in the Grove
Sit outdoors or on the patio to really get the most out of happy hour, lunch, and brunch especially *(see p113)*.

5 Front Porch Café
Serving one of the best breakfasts in Miami Beach, Front Porch *(see p88)* has a pleasant outdoor terrace, ideal for sipping cocktails and people-watching.

6 Mango's Tropical Café
One of the hottest action venues on South Beach, where you can enjoy live music and dancing, Floribbean dishes, and free-flowing cocktails *(see p88)*.

7 Love Life Café
Located in the Wynwood Arts District, this vegan café has a bright, spacious interior. It is known for its superb veggie burgers and jackfruit tacos.

8 Books and Books
Don't let the quietness deceive you; this is a very happening place *(see p112)*.

9 Versailles
Soak up the old-school Cuban atmosphere over *café con leche* (Spanish coffee) and coconut flan *(see p97)*.

10 Mangoes, Key West
A restaurant, bar, and sidewalk café, located on a busy corner *(see p131)*.

🔟 Parks and Gardens

1 Flamingo Gardens

MAP D3 ▪ 3750 South Flamingo Rd, Davie/Fort Lauderdale ▪ Adm ▪ www. flamingogardens.org

These gardens began life in 1927 as a weekend retreat for the citrus-farming Wray family. The botanical gardens and wildlife and bird sanctuary are worth at least a half-day visit. There's a "free-flight" aviary, featuring a mass of Florida birds, including the comical roseate spoonbill and, of course, the flamingo. A native butterfly and nectar-plant conservatory opened in 2023.

Flamingo Gardens resident

2 Pinecrest Gardens

This thoroughly enjoyable place features over 1,000 kinds of tropical plants, an art gallery, and an amphitheater for concerts and shows. There are also plenty of activities here *(see p58)* for children.

3 Fairchild Tropical Botanic Garden

One of the best of South Florida's ravishing tropical gardens *(see p115)* dotted with artificial lakes and a large collection of rare plants.

Fairchild Tropical Botanic Garden

4 Tropical Audubon Society

MAP F4 ▪ 5530 Sunset Dr

With a mission is to restore Florida's ecosystems, visitors are invited to explore the Doc Thomas House, the Steinberg Nature Center, and acres of lush hardwood hammock habitats and pine rockland.

5 Morikami Museum and Japanese Gardens

MAP D3 ▪ 4000 Morikami Park Rd, Delray Beach ▪ 561 495 0233 ▪ Adm ▪ www.morikami.org

Blossoming from a Japanese colony founded here in 1905, the Yamato-kan villa is surrounded by formal Japanese gardens of various ages: a Heian (9th- to 12th-century) *shinden*-style garden, a paradise garden emulating those of the 13th–14th centuries, rock gardens, a flat garden, and a modern romantic garden.

6 Miami Beach Botanical Garden

MAP R2 ▪ 2000 Convention Center Dr, Miami Beach ▪ 305 673 7256 ▪ www. mbgarden.org

This 3-acre (1.2-ha) oasis flaunts a Japanese Garden, Edible Garden

(with papayas, pineapples, and the like), and a palm garden. After admiring the orchids and flowering trees, take a walk along the promenade that shadows Collins Canal.

7 Fruit & Spice Park

Located in the Redland District south of Coconut Grove, this is the only tropical botanical garden *(see p115)* of its kind in the United States. The non-native plants are grouped by country of origin, and the tropical climate here sustains over 180 varieties of mango, 40 of banana, and 15 of jackfruit. The vast, lush park also houses the largest bamboo collection in the US. In the gift store you'll find imported fruit products, including dried and canned fruit, juices, jams, teas, and unusual seeds.

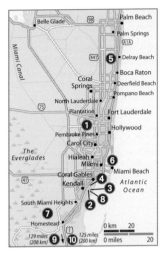

Crop display at the Fruit & Spice Park

8 Montgomery Botanical Center

This nonprofit botanical center *(see p115)*, accessible by appointment only, holds a vast collection of plants from across the globe.

9 Nancy Forrester's Secret Garden

MAP A6 ■ 518 Elizabeth St, Key West ■ 305 294 0015 ■ Adm

Lose yourself in this impossibly lush acre of land just a block off Duval Street. Intensely beautiful, the garden exudes a sense of peace and contentment. The ravishing varieties of flora – orchids, bromeliads, rare palms – and the well-loved parrots put any visitor at ease.

10 Key West Tropical Forest & Botanical Garden

MAP A6 ■ 5210 College Rd, Key West ■ 305 296 1504 ■ Adm ■ www.key west.garden

Established in 1936, this is the only frost-free, sub-tropical botanical garden in the continental US, and is home to endangered species. Trails and boardwalks wind through the 15-acre (6-ha) reserve, showcasing flora native to Florida Keys, Cuba, and the Caribbean. It's known for it's "champion trees", among them a saffron plum and cinnamon bark. With two wetland habitats and two dedicated butterfly gardens, it's also a haven for migratory birds and tropical butterflies.

Scenic lake, Key West Botanical Garden

Beaches

1 Bill Baggs Cape Florida State Park

Home to a historic 19th-century lighthouse, this pristine beach (see p82) is located at the southern tip of Key Biscayne.

2 Crandon Park

One of several South Florida beaches (see p82) rated among the top ten in the US, this one is on upper Key Biscayne.

Beautiful Crandon Park Beach

3 South Pointe Park Beach

MAP S6

Though not well known for its beaches, South Pointe Park's northern part is frequented by surfers, and you can watch cruise ships gliding in and out of the Port of Miami. It's also great for walks, and there's a fitness course, an observation tower, charcoal grills, picnic spots, and playgrounds.

4 Bahia Honda State Park

With two award-winning beaches, Calusa and Sandspur, Bahia Honda (see p121) is celebrated for its perfect white sands, abundance of watersports, and tropical forests.

5 Key West Beaches

MAP A6

Key West's relatively modest beaches are strung out along the southern side of the island, stretching from Fort Zachary Taylor Historic State Park in the west to Smathers Beach in the east. The latter is the largest and most popular, but locals favor the former because it's less crowded. For convenience, the beach at the bottom of Duval Street, at the Southernmost Point in the US, is fine, friendly, and offers several good refreshment options.

6 Hobie Island Beach and Virginia Key Beach

MAP H3

While Hobie Beach is popular with windsurfers, Virginia Key – neighbor to Key Biscayne and similarly shrouded in Australian pines – has no residents and few visitors. Under Old South segregation, it was the only Miami beach African Americans were allowed to use. Once you walk through the vegetation, the 2-mile (3-km) beach here is fine and relatively empty. Both are excellent for children due to the warm bay waters, but Virginia Key has deep waters and possible undertow.

Aerial vista of Lummus Park Beach

7 Lummus Park Beach
MAP S3

This stretch of sand – broad, long, and well-maintained – is, for many, the epitome of South Beach. During holiday season, you'll see hordes of sunbathers, some with boom boxes blasting, others just leisurely catching the rays. The more active play volleyball, do gymnastics, and, of course, take to the waves.

8 Sunny Isles Beach

More noteworthy for its 1950s tourist-resort kitsch than for its rocky sand, this developing strip (see p99) is popular with older tourists, as well as surfers and sailors. The souvenir shops and hotels that fringe the beach indulge in striking architectural fancies and mementos. You'll find the majority of stores on Collins (A1A) between 175th and 193rd streets.

9 Haulover Park Beach
MAP H1

Located just north of Bal Harbour, Haulover has been spared the sight of high-rise development. Noted for its clear blue waters, the dune-backed beach lies along the eastern side of the park. To the north is a clothing optional stretch – the only nude beach in the county.

10 Matheson Hammock Park Beach
MAP G4

North of Fairchild Tropical Botanic Garden, this beautiful 100-acre (40-ha) park was developed in the 1930s by Commodore J. W. Matheson. It features the human-made Atoll Pool, a saltwater swimming pool encircled by sand and palm trees and flushed naturally by nearby Biscayne Bay. The tranquil beach is popular with families and enjoys warm, safe waters surrounded by tropical hardwood forests. Other attractions include walking trails through the mangrove swamp.

Matheson Hammock Park Beach

TOP 10 Sports and Outdoor Activities

Playing beach volleyball

1 Volleyball
On every beach in South Florida, you'll find volleyball nets and likely team members ready to go. This is the quintessential beach sport *(see p84)*, where taking a tumble in the sand is part of the fun.

2 In-line Skating
Gliding along on little wheels is probably the number one activity for the perennially tanned of South Florida. Down on flaunt-it-all South Beach, you can rent in-line skates or get fitted for your very own pair.

3 Golf
You'll get endless opportunities to play golf throughout South Florida, making it a premier golfing-holiday destination. Many larger resorts have their own courses, too, but one of the best in the Greater Miami area is Crandon Golf Course *(see p84)*, which is the only public course on Key Biscayne.

4 Cycling
This is an excellent way to explore South Beach, Key Biscayne, or Key West *(see p84)*. Rental shops abound, and there are a good number of excellent bike trails in the Everglades, too.

5 Fishing
Reward Fishing Fleet: www. fishingmiami.com ■ AWS Charters: keywestflatsfishin.com ■ Good Times Key West: www.goodtimeskeywest. com ■ Fishing Headquarters: www. fishheadquarters.com

There are any number of companies that will organize deep-sea fishing excursions; for good freshwater fishing you should head to Amelia Earhart Park or Lake Okeechobee.

6 Swimming
Miami and the Keys are home to some of the most beautiful beaches in the US. Head to Bahia Honda State Park *(see p121)* for pristine sandy beaches where you can enjoy the warm, clear blue waters of the Atlantic Ocean and Florida Bay.

7 Surfing and Windsurfing
Miami has good prevailing winds and both calm and surging waters – so there is plenty of scope for good surfing and windsurfing *(see p84)*. The Keys tend to be good for windsurfing only, as the surrounding reefs break the big waves *(see p126)*.

8 Tennis
South Floridians love this game, and there are public and

private courts (see p84) everywhere. Key Biscayne is the top choice, while the Miami Open is held at Hard Rock Stadium every March.

9 Jet-Skiing and Parasailing

Sunset Watersports: sunsetwatersports keywest.com ■ **Sebago Watersports:** keywestsebago.com ■ **Fury Water Adventures:** www.furycat.com

Not as challenging as they may appear and, of course, great fun. In Miami, the placid intracoastal waterways are suitable for both, but it's the Keys that have the best conditions for these adventure sports, especially Key West (see p126).

Kayaking around the Keys

10 Boating and Kayaking

Blue Planet Kayak: 305 809 8110; www.blue-planet-kayak.com

Strike out on your own in a kayak and explore the colorful waters around the Keys, or the mangrove creeks off Florida Bay. Alternatively, you could enjoy an ecotour of the diverse marine life and some of the best birding in the country.

Teeing off, Crandon Golf Course

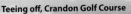

TOP 10 SPECTATOR SPORTS

Baseball game at Marlins Park

1 Baseball
501 Marlins Way
Two-time world champions Miami Marlins play at LoanDepot Park.

2 Jai Alai
Casino Miami, 3500 NW 37th Ave
Often called the world's fastest game.

3 Football
Hard Rock Stadium, 347 Don Shula Dr
Miami's contender in the National Football League is the Miami Dolphins.

4 Soccer
1350 NW 55th St, Fort Lauderdale
The DRV PNK Stadium hosts Miami's top MLS team, Inter Miami CF.

5 NASCAR racing
1 Speedway Blvd
Founded by Ralph Sanchez, Homestead Miami Speedway hosts several big events every year.

6 Tennis
Hard Rock Stadium, 347 Don Shula Dr
The Miami Open is one of the world's biggest non-Grand Slam tournaments.

7 Polo
3667 120th Ave S, Wellington
Popular around Palm Beach County, including at the National Polo Center.

8 Basketball
601 Biscayne Blvd
The Miami Heat calls the Miami-Dade Arena home.

9 Ice Hockey
FLA Live Arena, 1 Panther Parkway, Sunrise
Local team the Florida Panthers play out by the Everglades.

10 The Honda Classic
PGA National Resort and Spa, Palm Beach Gardens
This pro-golf tournament on the PGA Tour is held annually between February and March.

TOP 10 Snorkeling and Diving

3 Biscayne National Park

Closer to Miami than John Pennekamp, this location (see p116) has as many good snorkeling possibilities. You'll find vivid coral reefs to dive among, and mangrove swamps to explore by canoe.

4 Key Biscayne Parks

Both Crandon and Bill Baggs Parks (see p82) have great areas for snorkeling, in Miami's cleanest, clearest waters.

1 Looe Key National Marine Sanctuary

This is a brilliant coral dive location, and the closest great snorkeling to Key West. Access from Bahia Honda State Park (see p121).

2 John Pennekamp Coral Reef State Park

This park (see p121) offers some of the best snorkeling in the world. Boats can also be rented here, or you can take a glass-bottomed boat.

The beach at Fort Zachary Taylor

5 Key West Waters
MAP A6

Take the plunge right off the beach at Fort Zachary Taylor Historic State Park, or join an expedition out to the reefs that lie around this island (see pp32–3). Plenty of trips are offered by local companies, most of them taking three to four hours in total, including at least an hour and a half of reef time. They usually leave twice a day, at around 9am and again around 1pm.

6 Bahia Honda State Park Waters

The beautiful, sandy beach of Bahia Honda (see p121) in the Keys – often lauded as one of the best beaches in the US – has excellent waters for swimming and snorkeling. Equipment rentals are available here.

Statue, John Pennekamp Coral Reef

7 Red Reef Park

Gumbo Limbo Nature Center: MAP D3; 1801 North Ocean Blvd, Boca Raton; 561 544 8605; open 9am–4pm Tue–Sun (from noon Mon); www.gumbolimbo.org

Boca Raton is famous for its extensive and beautifully maintained parks, and this offers some of the area's best beaches and snorkeling. An artificial reef can provide hours of undersea viewing and is suitable for youngsters. The Gumbo Limbo Nature Center is just across the street.

8 Islamorada

MAP C5

Halfway along the Keys, Islamorada is a superb base for snorkeling and diving trips. The nearby Crocker and Alligator reefs provide habitats for a wide variety of marine life. The shipwrecks of the *Eagle* and the *Cannabis Cruiser* are home to gargantuan amberjack and grouper.

9 Dry Tortugas National Park

Found about 70 miles (110 km) west of Key West, these seven islands and their surrounding waters make a fantastic park *(see p133)*. The snorkeling sights are exceptional, due to the shallow waters and abundance of marine life. You can snorkel directly off the beaches of Fort Jefferson or go to the wreck of the *Windjammer*, which sank on Loggerhead Reef in 1907. Tropical fish, goliath grouper, and lobster can be spotted.

Diving in waters off Fort Lauderdale

10 Fort Lauderdale Waters

Sea Experience: MAP D3; 954 770 3483; www.seaxp.com

Fort Lauderdale has been awarded the Blue Wave Beaches certification for spotless sands and crystal clear waters, which add up to superior underwater viewing. Many of the most interesting parts of the three-tiered natural reef system here are close to the shore, although most require a short boat ride. In addition, more than 80 artificial reefs have been built to enhance the growth of marine flora and fauna. Sea Experience is just one of several companies organizing snorkeling and scuba trips off this coastline.

The 19th-century Fort Jefferson on Garden Key, Dry Tortugas National Park

TOP 10 Off the Beaten Path

The calm sea from the Kampong

sand, salvaged from a refugee boat, while above it a mural depicts the history of the Catholic Church in Cuba. The shrine is dedicated to Our Lady of Charity, the Cuban patron saint (the statue inside is a replica of the revered original from the shrine in El Cobre).

1 The Kampong

One of Miami's lesser-visited gems, this tropical garden (see p109) is sited southwest of downtown Coconut Grove. The former estate of horticulturalist David Fairchild, it holds an impressive collection of tropical flowers, fruit trees, and plants.

2 Ermita de la Caridad Church, Coconut Grove

MAP M5 ▪ 3609 S Miami Ave, Coconut Grove ▪ 305 854 2404 ▪ Open 7am–9pm Mon–Sat (to 7pm Sun)

Built in the late 1960s, this peculiar conical church is the religious heart of expat Cuban life. Beneath the altar there's a cache of Cuban soil and

3 Los Pinareños Fruteria

This fruit stand and outdoor café (see p96) in the heart of Little Havana seems transported straight from Cuba. Afro-Cuban tunes waft through boxes of papaya, oranges, guavas, and coconuts, while plates of delicious chicken rice and fresh juices are doled out from the kitchen.

4 Overtown

MAP G3 ▪ Lyric Theater 819 NW 2nd Ave ▪ 786 708 4610 ▪ www.bahlt.org

Miami's African American community thrived in this segregated neighborhood after the incorporation of the city in 1896. Remnants of the area's glory days include the beautifully renovated Lyric Theater, opened in 1913. It acts as a cultural center today, home to the Black Archives museum.

5 Santería and Vodou Botánicas

For an insight into the practice of the hybrid Caribbean religious of Santeria (p19) and Vodou (or Voodoo) – West

Ermita de la Caridad Church

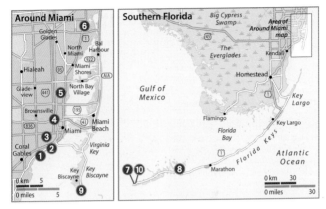

African ritual and belief blended with Roman Catholicism – visit the *botánicas* (traditional folk medicine shops) in Little Haiti. These stores carry all sorts of potions, candles, statuary, and glass jars packed with herbs.

6 Ancient Spanish Monastery

MAP H1 ■ 16711 W Dixie Hwy, North Miami Beach ■ 305 945 1461

Built in 1133 near Segovia, this monastery was occupied by Cistercian monks for almost 700 years. In 1925 it was aquired by the publisher William Randolph Hearst, who had the building shipped to the US in more than 11,000 crates. The structure languished in warehouse until it was bought by the Episcopalian church in 1964. Today it serves a growing congregation and attracts many visitors.

7 Nancy Forrester's Secret Garden, Key West

Local artist Nancy Forrester and her friends began working on this lush, funky, and indefinable Key West garden *(see p49)* in the 1970s.

8 No Name Pub

MAP B6 ■ 30813 Watson Blvd, Big Pine Key ■ www.nonamepub.com

This no-frills bar and restaurant *(see p77)* started as a 1930s general store, before the pub was added in 1936. It is best known for its "pub pizza".

9 Stiltsville, Key Biscayne

MAP H4 ■ www.stiltsville trust.org

Drive to the southernmost tip of Key Biscayne, look way out over the water, and you'll spy seven fragile-looking structures built on stilts. These fishermen's bungalows are the last of what was once a much larger community from the 1930s to 1960s. Their number has dwindled due to hurricanes, and the site is now overseen by the Stiltsville Trust (public access is by permit only).

Wooden house out at sea, Stiltsville

10 "The Garden of Eden," Key West

MAP A6 ■ The Bull and Whistle Bar, 3/F, 224 Duval St, Key West ■ 305 296 4565 ■ Open noon–3am daily ■ www.bullkeywest.org

Devoted nudists can find an appreciative milieu in this renowned bar *(see p130)*, as well as within the walls and gardens of many guest-houses scattered around town.

📷10 Children's Attractions

1 The Key West Butterfly and Nature Conservatory

MAP A6 ▪ 1316 Duval St, Key West ▪ 305 296 2988 ▪ Open 9am–4:30pm daily ▪ Adm ▪ www.keywestbutterfly.com

Take a magical stroll through the conservatory filled with hundreds of beautiful butterflies, flowering plants, trees, birds, and cascading waterfalls in this climate-controlled, glass-enclosed habitat.

2 Pinecrest Gardens

MAP F4 ▪ 11000 Red Rd, Pinecrest ▪ Open 9am–5pm daily ▪ Adm ▪ www.pinecrestgardens.org

There's plenty for kids to enjoy here: a Splash N Play area, mangrove forest, colorful playground, domino games, and a giant chess and checkers board, along with children's theater performances, concerts, and movies.

Facade of Miami Children's Museum

3 Miami Children's Museum

MAP G3 ▪ 980 MacArthur Causeway ▪ 305 373 5437 ▪ Open 10am–1:30pm & 2:30–6pm daily ▪ Adm ▪ www.miamichildrensmuseum.org

Play, learn, imagine, and create at this museum. Interactive exhibits related to the arts, culture, and communication are on offer. Catch a fish in the waterfall or take a trip on a pretend cruise ship complete with portholes.

4 Amelia Earhart Park

MAP G2 ▪ 401 E 65th St, Hialeah ▪ 305 685 8389 ▪ Open sunrise–sunset daily

Come to this park for a fun and wholesome family day out. There's a watersports complex with wake-surfing and waterskiing, bike rentals, hiking and mountain biking trails, volleyball courts, and soccer-fields. There are playgrounds and fish-filled lakes as well. The whole park is delightfully uncrowded, as it is well away from the tourist track.

5 Turtle Hospital

MAP B6 ▪ 2396 Overseas Hwy, Marathon ▪ 305 743 2552 ▪ Open 9am–6pm daily ▪ Adm ▪ www.turtlehospital.org

Based on Key Vaca, the Turtle Hospital is a rescue, rehabilitation, and release facility for injured turtles recovered from all over the Keys. Since its opening in 1986, it has successfully treated and released more than 2,000 turtles. There are guided tours of the hospital and rehabilitation sections where you can meet some of the current patients too, which is a great highlight for kids. It also houses several permanent residents deemed unreleasable by the Florida Wildlife Commission.

Kids enjoying MeLaβ at the Phillip and Patricia Frost Museum of Science

6 Phillip and Patricia Frost Museum of Science

MAP G3 ▪ 1101 Biscayne Blvd ▪ 305 434 9600 ▪ Open 10am–6pm daily ▪ Adm ▪ www.frostscience.org

The young and curious will find much to capture their attention and imagination here. There are over 140 hands-on exhibits to explore the worlds of sound, light, and gravity. Head to the "MeLaβ", which focuses on health and wellbeing, or "Crush the Calories" a digital gaming installation. Outside – beyond the collections of fossils, mounted insects, spiders, and butterflies – lies the Wildlife Center, home to birds, tortoises, and enormous snakes. The planetarium offers laser light shows set to rock music.

7 HistoryMiami Museum

The Downtown museum (see p43) has a number of hands-on activities and multimedia programs, such as an exploration of the past and present ecology of the Everglades.

8 Cape Florida Light

Older kids love clambering up this 95-ft- (30-m-) high lighthouse (children under-8 are not permitted to go up), while the surrounding beaches of Bill Baggs Cape Florida State Park (see p82) are entertaining for the whole family.

9 Hobie Island Beach

An excellent stretch of beach (see p50), popular with windsurfers and also with families appreciative of its calm, shallow waters.

10 Boat Tours Biscayne Bay

MAP P1 ▪ Island Queen Cruises, 401 Biscayne Blvd, Bayside Marketplace ▪ 844 215 6546 ▪ Every hour 11am–5pm daily ▪ www.islandqueencruises.com

Narrated boat tours are the best way to see the islands of Biscayne Bay – the tranquil stretch of water between Downtown and Miami Beach – which is dominated by opulent mansions owned by celebrities such as Shaquille O'Neal and Oprah Winfrey.

Boat sightseeing tour, Biscayne Bay

🔟 Performing Arts Venues

Entrance to the Colony Theatre

1 Colony Theatre
MAP Q2 ▪ 1040 Lincoln Rd, Miami Beach ▪ 305 674 1040 ▪ www.miaminewdrama.org

Enjoy the city's best music, dance, comedy, and theatre performances here. It's also home to Miami New Drama, a non-profit theater company.

2 Kravis Center
MAP D2 ▪ 701 Okeechobee Blvd, W Palm Beach ▪ 561 832 7469 ▪ www.kravis.org

This performing arts center houses the Palm Beach Opera and Palm Beach Pops. It also has a concert hall, the Rinker Playhouse, the Helen K. Persson Hall and the Cohen Pavilion ballroom and events hall.

3 Miracle Theatre
MAP G3 ▪ 280 Miracle Mile, Coral Gables ▪ 305 444 9293 ▪ www.actorsplayhouse.org

The 1940s Deco-style movie theater was converted into a playhouse in 1995 and has won accolades for musicals such as *West Side Story*.

4 Olympia Theater
The Olympia Theater *(see p95)*, located in Downtown Miami, is a major venue offering a varied program of plays, music, dance, and film.

5 Adrienne Arsht Center for the Performing Arts
MAP G3 ▪ 1300 Biscayne Blvd ▪ 305 949 6722 ▪ www.arshtcenter.org

This spectacular complex includes three state-of-the-art theaters, the Ziff Ballet Opera House, Knight Concert Hall, and a restored Art Deco tower.

6 Broward Center
MAP D3 ▪ 201 SW 5th Ave, Fort Lauderdale ▪ 954 462 0222 ▪ www.browardcenter.org

Major arts center in Fort Lauderdale, opened in 1991 at the heart of the Riverwalk Arts and Entertainment District. Key partners include the Symphony of the Americas, Florida Grand Opera, and Miami City Ballet.

Dreyfoos Hall, the largest venue at the Kravis Center

7 Wertheim Performing Arts Center

MAP F3 ▪ 10910 SW 17th St ▪ www.carta.fiu.edu/the-wertheim

West of Downtown on the campus of Florida International University, this state-of-the-art venue comprises the Mainstage Theatre, the Concert Hall, and the Black Box Studio Theatre. It is also home to the FIU School of Music and Department of Theatre.

8 The Fillmore Miami Beach at the Jackie Gleason Theater

MAP R2 ▪ 1700 Washington Ave, Miami Beach ▪ www.fillmoremb.com

Currently undergoing renovation until 2025, the Jackie Gleason Theater is famed for hosting a variety of performances.

New World Symphony concert

9 New World Center

MAP R2 ▪ 500 17th St, Miami Beach ▪ 305 673 3330 ▪ www.nws.edu

Home to the New World Symphony, which is made up of music college graduates. The young virtuosos perform gospel, Piazzolla tango, symphonies, and chamber works.

10 Miami-Dade County Auditorium

MAP G3 ▪ 2901 W Flagler St ▪ 305 547 5414 ▪ www.miamidadecounty auditorium.org

Built in 1951, this Deco-style venue is proud to have been one of the first in the country to host the late Luciano Pavarotti, when he was still a virtual unknown. Operas, concerts, and touring events all benefit from the excellent acoustics in the auditorium.

TOP 10 ENTERTAINERS FROM MIAMI

Cher, a former SoBe resident

1 Cher
You can see where the iconic singer lived with Sonny on the water in Fort Lauderdale and South Beach.

2 Don Johnson
The star of *Miami Vice*, this King of 1980s Cool helped put hip "new" South Beach on the map *(see p83)*.

3 Jackie Gleason
"The Great One," who practically invented early American television, brought his *Jackie Gleason Show* permanently to Miami in 1964.

4 Madonna
"The Queen of Pop" once owned a piece of the Delano Hotel restaurant.

5 Dave Barry
The newspaper humorist and author has helped to create Miami's image as an over-the-top urban free-for-all.

6 Gloria Estefan
The symbol of unstoppable Cuban Power for many, this pop songstress has succeeded in building an impressive cultural and real-estate empire.

7 Rosie O'Donnell
The talkshow hostess calls West Palm Beach home and is involved in local politics.

8 Jennifer Lopez
This Latin American actress and songstress has owned a mansion and estate at Miami Beach since 2002.

9 Flo Rida
The rapper grew up in Greater Miami and still lives in the area.

10 Tito Puente, Jr.
The talented musician and son of the famed Latin bandleader has made South Florida home, where he promotes LGBTQ+ causes.

LGBTQ+ Venues

1 Beach at 12th Street, SoBe
MAP S3–4

This beautiful sandy stretch of SoBe, with its rainbow flags flying, is one of the most popular beaches among the LGBTQ+ community.

Beach at Fort Lauderdale

2 Fort Lauderdale LGBTQ+ Beaches
MAP D3

Two major beaches in the Fort Lauderdale area are LGBTQ+ friendly, and particularly popular with gay men: Sebastian Street Beach; and Dr. Von D. Mizell-Eula Johnson State Park.

3 Haulover Park Beach, Miami Beach
MAP H1

Everyone is welcome at this pristine stretch of shoreline. The northern portion is a designated nude area where clothing is very much optional.

4 Pride Center at Equality Park
MAP D3 ■ 2040 N Dixie Hwy, Wilton Manors ■ 954 463 9005

Located a few miles north of Fort Lauderdale, in the town of Wilton Manors (one of South Florida's biggest LGBTQ+ towns), this is a well-maintained center. There's an extensive library of LGBTQ+ literature and reference works, friendly and helpful staff, a full calendar of special events, and plenty of opportunities for lively social interaction.

5 The Pub Wilton Manors
MAP D3 ■ 2283 Wilton Dr, Wilton Manors ■ 754 200 5244 ■ Open 8am–2am daily ■ www.thepubwm.com

This is another Wilton Manors mainstay, beloved for its open-air patio, all-day two-for-one "happy hour," and dancing until 2am. Drag shows take place several nights a week and fun karaoke and trivia nights are hosted on Wednesdays.

Vendors and picnic tables on Wilton Drive, Wilton Manors

There are other events and variety shows every night.

6 Shoppes of Wilton Manors, Broward County
MAP D3 ■ 2262 Wilton Dr

The "gayborhood" of Wilton Manors is home to LGBTQ+-friendly businesses, the Stonewall National Museum and Archives, and the annual Stonewall Pride Festival.

7 Georgie's Alibi Monkey Bar
MAP D3 ■ 2266 Wilton Dr, Wilton Manors ■ www.alibiwiltonmanors.com

This restaurant, sports bar, and video bar opened in 1997 in what was a rundown area, but Wilton Manors has since blossomed and this bar has flourished with it. The Alibi is one of South Florida's best LGBTQ+ venues, serving American classics, with affordable nightly drink specials.

8 Ramrod, Fort Lauderdale
MAP D3 ■ 1508 NE 4th Ave ■ 954 763 8219

Fort Lauderdale's Ramrod is a leather and uniform bar with a welcoming crowd. The place is packed on Friday and Saturday nights. There's usually a line at the door, but it's worth the wait. Fantastic DJs make this a great party scene, and on some Saturdays they host intro nights to queer leather and kink.

9 LGBT+ Visitor Center
MAP D3 ■ 1130 Washington Ave, South Beach ■ 305 397 8914

Set in the Old City Hall, Miami's LGBT+ center offers information, publications, and free Wi-Fi. It hosts great events, and also helps with last-minute hotel bookings, tours, dinner reservations, and recommendations.

10 Key West Business Guild

Established in 1978, this LGBTQ+ organization operates the Gay Key West Visitor Center (see p129) at 808 Duval Street. It has information about the island, local businesses, area attractions and events such as Tropical Heat, Key West Pride, Key West Womenfest, and the Headdress Ball.

The Gay Key West Visitor Center

Nightlife

The hip interior of Mynt

Mynt

Enjoy a menu of custom cocktails at this vibrant, hot night-spot *(see p87)* in South Beach. The flashy crowd here, including the celebrity elite, enjoy partying in style to house and hip-hop, although there is no real dance floor.

2 Watr at the Rooftop

Atop the trendy 1 Hotel, Watr *(see p87)* is decked out in reclaimed wood and draws a trendy crowd with its relaxed, breezy vibe, and expansive 18th-floor views across South Beach. There's also a menu of Peruvian-Japanese snacks.

Travis Scott performing at E11EVEN

3 Twist

SoBe's premier LGBTQ+ venue *(see p86)* is enormous, hugely popular, and always jumping, but it doesn't get started until very late, of course, and then it goes till dawn. Don't show up before midnight unless you want to be considered a desperate wallflower.

4 Salsa Mia

MAP S4 ▪ 900 Ocean Dr ▪ 305 458 4558 ▪ www.salsamia.com
If you want an active outing, try the two-hour Salsa class and learn to sway to the sizzling sound of a live band performing Miami's signature music. Dance lessons and party packages are available until 5 in the morning.

5 Escape Lounge

MAP D3 ▪ 300 SW 1st Ave, Fort Lauderdale ▪ Open until 4am Fri–Sun ▪ www.escapelounge.club
This glamorous club and lounge bar is a popular choice in Fort Lauderdale. It is known for its free Latin nights on Saturdays, and "2 for 1 drinks for ladies" on Fridays.

6 E11EVEN Miami

MAP G3 ▪ 29 NE 11th St ▪ www.11miami.com
Located in Downtown Miami's entertainment strip, this vast, luxurious club hosts a roster of

in-house performers and top DJs. The rooftop restaurant offers a variety of late-night munchies.

7 El Patio
MAP G3 ▪ 167 NW 23rd St ▪ 786 409 2241 ▪ www.elpatiowynwood.com

This south-of-the-border-style venue plays throbbing Reggae and Latin music, and offers deals during happy hours and a ladies' night on Tuesdays. There are live performances too.

Partygoers on the beach, Nikki Beach

8 Nikki Beach Miami
This beachfront complex is a playground for the Euro-hip and trendy denizens of SoBe. Nikki Beach (see p87) is located on the first floor and Club 01 is on the second. There are new themes and dances every week, fashion shows, and interactive entertainment.

9 Basement
Rub shoulders with Hollywood glitterati at one of Miami's hottest micro-clubs (see p87). This hip party spot has a strobe-lit dance floor, a bowling alley, and a mini ice-skating rink all of which add to its retro, Studio 54 vibe.

10 Treehouse
This Miami Beach club (see p87) is all about the dancing, with simple decor and a kaleidoscopic dance floor where international and local DJs pump out house and techno until the early hours. There is an outdoor terrace and many corners, where one can relax.

Restaurants

The busy counter of the Cuban restaurant El Rey De Las Fritas

1 El Rey De Las Fritas

Sit and dine at the counter or in one of the retro booths of this iconic Little Havana canteen *(see p97)*. It specializes in *fritas* (Cuban-style burgers topped with shoestring fries). It also serves cheese sticks, corn fritters, coconut flan, and empanadas.

2 Michael's Genuine Food and Drink

Chef and owner Michael Schwartz provides passion on every plate at this award-winning neighborhood gem *(see p103)*. Pizza from the wood-burning oven is especially good.

3 Caffe Abbracci, Coral Gables

Enjoy tasty Italian cuisine at this local favorite. The formal ambience of this restaurant *(see p113)* makes it perfect for a special occasion. Try the lobster-filled ravioli or the gnocchi in an *amatriciana* (pork cheek and tomato) sauce.

4 Barton G – The Restaurant, Miami Beach

Exquisitely presented food can be enjoyed here in the pleasant orchid garden or the stylish bar. Barton G *(see p89)* knows how to do relaxed elegance really well.

5 Stubborn Seed

Owned by Jeremy Ford, a *Top Chef* winner, this creative restaurant *(see p89)* is known for its exceptional eight-course tasting menu featuring seasonal dishes. The dinner tasting menu features dishes such as charred Japanese yellow tail crudo and confit duck tortellini with winter truffle. You can also sit at the bar to sample snacks *à la carte*.

6 Joe's Stone Crab, South Beach

A popular South Beach restaurant *(see p89)* that is always packed with diners – you might need to reserve a table well in advance. Located on Washington Avenue, it's consistently excellent, although considered a bit too touristy for some people. It is closed from August to mid-October during crab off-season.

Jumbo claws at Joe's Stone Crab

7 CVI.CHE 105

Contemporary Peruvian restaurant *(see p97)* helmed by Juan Chipoco. Best known for its exceptionally fresh and zesty ceviches, the restaurant occupies a chic space adorned with eclectic artwork.

8 Fontana

Found in the prestigious Biltmore, this elegant restaurant *(see p113)* takes Italian fine dining to an entirely new level. Expect the freshest seafood, locally sourced ingredients, and a near-perfect wine list.

9 Versailles, Little Havana

Everybody's favorite Cuban hub is a must-stop on a visit to Little Havana – this is a busy, rambunctious place. The restaurant *(see p97)* offers traditional Cuban fare and a convivial atmosphere, and there is a bakery next-door too.

Diners at Versailles

10 Le Bouchon du Grove, Coconut Grove

Loved by locals, this friendly and relaxed French bistro *(see p113)* is always jam-packed with customers at lunchtime. Colorful posters on the wall, freshly baked croissants, and delicious desserts make this cozy spot one of the best places for a casual meal. Outside tables are at a premium for a view of the busy main street.

TOP 10 FLORIBBEAN FOOD AND DRINK

Blackened grouper

1 Blackened Grouper
Having your fish cooked "blackened" is a Cajun recipe that has caught on in most restaurants in South Florida.

2 Conch Chowder or Fritters
The snail- or slug-like creature that lives in beautiful pink shells is served up in a traditional, rather chewy dish.

3 Black Beans and Rice
"Moros y Cristianos" (black beans and rice) is the staple of the Cuban diet. Its savory, smoky flavor complements almost everything.

4 Yucca/Plantain Chips
The variations on bananas and potatoes are often served as deep-fried chips – slightly sweet and wonderfully aromatic.

5 Café Cubano (Cafecito)
A tiny cup of intensely sweet, black coffee; this is the mainstay of life for many. If you want it with a drop of milk, ask for a *cortadito*.

6 Ceviche
A seafood marinade using lime juice, onions, green bell peppers, and cilantro (coriander).

7 Lechon Asado
Pork is a big part of the Cuban diet. This term translates as "roast suckling pig," and is the ultimate feast.

8 Chimichurri
A sauce of olive oil, garlic, lemon juice or wine vinegar, and parsley. Jalapeño peppers are optional.

9 Key Lime Pie
The Key lime looks more like a lemon but makes the most exquisite pie.

10 Alfajores
A typical Cuban pastry composed of chocolate, custard, and coconut.

🔟 Chic Shopping Centers

2 Shops at Merrick Park

MAP G3 ▪ 358 San Lorenzo Ave, Coral Gables ▪ www.shop satmerrickpark.com

The Shops at Merrick Park offers luxury retail stores amid a posh urban garden ideal for concerts. At its heart are Neiman Marcus and Miami's first Nordstrom, along with fine restaurants, such as the elegant Perry's Steakhouse. The Mediterranean Revival style, with landscaped walkways and fountains, was pioneered by the city's founder George Merrick (see p25).

3 Las Olas Boulevard and the Galleria
MAP D3 ▪ 2414 E Sunrise Blvd, Fort Lauderdale ▪ www.galleriamall-fl.com

Fort Lauderdale's high-end shopping is spread between its main street downtown and a mall just near the beach. Las Olas's 100-plus boutiques are unique, and are interspersed with some really good restaurants. The Galleria (East Sunrise Blvd at A1A) offers an Apple Store and Macy's.

4 Worth Avenue, Palm Beach
The avenue offers marvelously expensive, ultra-exclusive must-haves for the rich and famous (see p30).

1 Bal Harbour Shops
MAP H2 ▪ 9700 Collins Ave ▪ Open 11am–10pm Mon–Sat, noon–6pm Sun ▪ www.bal harbourshops.com

The ultimate in chi-chi, down to the English spelling of "Harbour" (see p99), this is one of Miami's first high-fashion malls. It opened in 1965, and is now home to the likes of Dior, Hermès, Tiffany, and Prada, along with several fine dining options, all surrounded by tropical gardens.

High-end Bal Harbour Shops

Aventura Mall, illuminated at dusk

5 Aventura Mall
MAP H1 ■ 19501 Biscayne Blvd ■ 305 935 1110 ■ www.aventuramall.com

Department stores Bloomingdale's and Nordstrom are the upscale anchors at this mall that offers three levels of retail space. Specialty stores include Hugo Boss, Anthropologie, and Michael Kors. Art installations, some excellent restaurants and cafés, an international food court, and a 24-screen cineplex complete the picture.

6 Dadeland Mall
MAP F4 ■ 7535 N Kendall Dr ■ 305 665 6226 ■ www.simon.com/mall/dadeland-mall

Fear not – there is a Saks Fifth Avenue even way down in South Miami – plus some 170 high-end specialty stores and several other fine anchor stores, including the state's largest Macy's. Unless you're shopping on the cheap, ignore the fact that there's also JC Penney, Zara, and Footlocker. The decor is pleasing, if a bit predictable, with palm-tree pillars and ceilings painted to resemble the sky.

7 Collins Avenue from 6th to 9th Street, SoBe
This area (see p85) is great to stroll and shop. There are boutique hotels, cigar shops, and cafés interspersed with lower-priced stores such as Shoe Palace and Armani Exchange. A variety of price ranges makes this area one for the whole family to shop in.

8 The Falls
MAP F4 ■ 8888 SW 136th St ■ 305 255 4750 ■ www.simon.com/mall/the-falls

Semi-open-air arcades with waterfalls and tropical vegetation form the backdrop to over 100 shops. The stores here include Abercrombie & Fitch, Macy's, Coach, Sephora, and the Adventure Kids amusement area.

9 Town Center at Boca Raton
MAP D3 ■ Town Center 6000 W Glades Rd ■ 561 368 6000 ■ www.simon.com /mall/town-center-at-boca-raton

Boca's premier mall has been expanded, and has taken a quantum leap into even greater luxury. Set amid tropical foliage, skylights, hand-glazed tiles, and sculptural accents, there's also a fancy cuisine court. Venture into downtown Boca and stroll through Mizner Park, where you'll find more chic shopping options.

Town Center at Boca Raton

10 Duval Street, Key West
MAP A6

Besides tacky T-shirt shops, Key West's main drag is home to superb emporiums of quality merchandise, including: clothing at Stitches of Key West (No. 533); shoes at Birkenstock (No. 612); local crafts at Key West Pottery (No. 1203); and African art and Persian rugs at Archeo Gallery (No. 1208).

Malls and Markets

1 Sawgrass Mills Mall
MAP D3 ■ 12801 W Sunrise Blvd, Flamingo Rd ■ 954 846 2350 ■ www.simon.com/mall/sawgrass-mills

This is one of the country's largest outlet and retail centers, which you'll learn as you drive its circumference trying to find the way in. This 8-acre (3-ha) mall comprises more than 350 discount outlets, from high-fashion brands to value retailers.

Bayside Marketplace in the evening

2 Bayside Marketplace
Chain boutiques abound in this sprawling marketplace (see p92), with the occasional trendy local shop adding spice. It holds a prime spot right on the waterfront.

3 Lincoln Road Markets
MAP R2 ■ Lincoln Rd, between Washington Ave & Alton Rd

A lively pedestrian area, graced with attractive fountains and upscale restaurants and shops, this also offers various markets. On Sunday, there's Lincoln Road Farmers' Market which sells regional products, and specialties. On most Sundays from October to May, there's also an Antique & Collectible Market that sells art, jewelry, furniture, clothing, and Miami memorabilia, between 8am and 5pm.

4 Time Out Market Miami
MAP H3 ■ 1601 Drexel Ave, Miami Beach ■ 786 753 5388 ■ timeout.com/miami/time-out-market

Opened after much anticipation and fanfare in 2018, this trendy food and cultural marketplace is located at a prime spot, just off Miami Beach's Lincoln Road. It features some of the city's top chefs and restauranteurs, such as Jeremy Ford, Micheal Beltran, and Alberto Cabera, all under one roof.

5 Los Pinareños Fruteria
Little Havana's foremost fruit and vegetable market (see p96) sells produce that can be difficult to find elsewhere, and you can get fresh juice, snacks, and flowers, too.

6 The Swap Shop
MAP D3 ■ 3291 W Sunrise Blvd, Fort Lauderdale ■ www.floridaswapshop.com

Eighty-eight acres (35 ha) of shopping at bargain prices, entertainment, and fun, the Swap Shop serves 12 million shoppers a year. This huge outdoor/indoor flea market features antiques, collectibles, clothing, plants, and a farmers' market. Inside, in addition to an international food court and a video arcade, there are also amusement rides. The complex claims to have the world's largest drive-in theater with 14 screens.

7 Dania Beach Historic Antiques District

MAP D3 ■ Federal Hwy 1 north for two blocks from Dania Beach Blvd

Here is South Florida's largest concentration of antiques shops. More than 100 dealers offer an array of furniture, fine art, and jewelry, as well as glass, pottery, and china, and various other collectibles. Prices vary greatly, so shop around for bargains.

8 Opa-Locka Flea Market

MAP G2 ■ 13449 NW 42nd Ave ■ https://opalockamarket.com

After the beloved old Opa-Locka/Hialeah Flea Market shuttered in 2022, it reopened in a new location up the street. Around 200 vendors occupy the slick, air-conditioned indoor space, with more spilling into the outdoor areas, selling a variety of accessories, clothing, decor, and more.

9 Española Way Market

MAP R3 ■ 15th St, South Beach

On Sundays, there's a small, rather esoteric market along Española Way, selling flowers, arts and crafts, and organic products. An array of vaguely hippie items also make an appearance, such as amulets, scented candles, stones, bric-a-brac, and clothing – all natural, of course. You can get your palm read, too, or decorated with henna if you prefer.

Ramblas walkway, Dolphin Mall

10 Dolphin Mall

MAP F3 ■ 11401 NW 12th St ■ 305 365 7446 ■ www.shopdolphinmall.com

More than 200 stores are crammed into one of Greater Miami's most popular middle-range malls. In part, this is an outlet for the heavy hitters including Saks Fifth Avenue, Brooks Brothers, and J. Crew, but there is also a good range of boutiques as well as a 19-screen cineplex at the heart of it all, on the "Ramblas," where a selection of lively restaurants are found.

Shoppers enjoying the weekend market on Española Way

Miami and the Keys for Free

Aerial view of the sands, South Beach

1 A Day on South Beach

With so much happening on land, it can be easy to neglect Miami's biggest free attraction – the beach itself (see pp12–13), and those famous candy-colored lifeguard towers.

2 Mallory Square Sunset Celebration, Key West

MAP A6 ▪ Mallory Square Dock, Key West ▪ Begins at sunset ▪ www.sunsetcelebration.org

Key West's Sunset Celebration started in the 1960s. Today these nightly gatherings feature arts and crafts, jugglers, fire-eaters, food carts, and cheap cocktails as a backdrop for the sinking of the sun.

3 Holocaust Memorial

Miami's moving tribute (see p38) to the Holocaust depicts a giant bronze arm tattooed with an Auschwitz number reaching toward the sky. The black marble walls around the sculpture are inscribed with the names of the victims of Nazi atrocities.

4 Miami Circle

MAP N2 ▪ Brickell Ave, Downtown

Just across the Brickell Avenue Bridge south of Downtown Miami, a small park preserves the ring of 24 holes known as the Miami Circle. The site was discovered by accident in 1998, and the prehistoric shell-tools found here were used to carbon-date the site to between 1,700 and 2,000 years old.

5 Tour the Wynwood Walls

MAP G3 ▪ 2520 NW 2nd Ave, between NW 25th and NW 26th Sts ▪ Open 11am–7pm Sun–Thu (to 8pm Fri & Sat) ▪ www.thewynwood walls.com

The Wynwood district (see p100) is crammed with art galleries and adorned with giant murals known as the Wynwood Walls. The main group lies on 2nd Avenue, just to the north of Downtown Miami.

Detail of a mural, Wynwood Walls

6 Institute of Contemporary Art

MAP G2 ■ 61 NE 41st St
■ Open 11am–6pm Wed–
Sun ■ www.icamiami.org

Miami's top contemporary art museum focuses on local, emerging, and under-recognized artists.

7 Stroll Along Lincoln Road Mall

Pedestrianized Lincoln Road Mall (see p82) is an upscale shopping strip lined with fashionable brand-name stores and alfresco cafés; Sunday afternoons are especially lively.

Palm-tree-lined Lincoln Road Mall

8 Cubaocho Museum

This dynamic Cuban American cultural center (see p93) hosts exhibits of Cuban art and a roster of live events. Visitors can also relax at a traditional café and a bar serving amazing mojitos.

9 Oldest House Museum, Key West

MAP A6 ■ 322 Duval St, Key West
■ 305 294 9501 ■ Open 10am–4pm
Mon–Sat ■ www.oirf.org

Built in 1829, this is the "oldest house" on Duval Street. The museum inside chronicles the history of Key West through family portraits, original furnishings, and historic ship models.

10 Observing Key Deer on Big Pine Key

MAP B6 ■ 305 872 0700 ■ Visitor center open 10am–3pm Wed–Fri
■ www.fws.gov/nationalkeydeer

Big Pine Key is known for its herds of feral Key deer. The best time to spot them is at sunrise or sunset.

TOP 10 BUDGET TIPS

Yoga enthusiasts, Bayfront Park

1 Free Yoga
Free yoga classes are offered daily at Bayfront Park and on Lincoln Rd.

2 Go to the beach
Beaches are free and open to the public, even if parking is not.

3 Monthly art walks
Visit Coral Gables and Wynwood when the free monthly art walks/gallery nights take place.

4 Free museums
Try to visit museums on free days, such as the Jewish Museum (Saturday) and The Wolfsonion-FIU (Friday nights).

5 Go Miami pass
Buy a Go Miami pass to enjoy exclusive discounts of up to 55 per cent at around 25 major attractions (www.gocity.com/miami).

6 Travel during off-peak season
To save money avoid traveling during the peak season. January to April is the most expensive time.

7 Take the bus
On arrival in Miami, save by taking the Miami Beach Airport Express bus rather than a taxi.

8 Rent a bike
Not only is cycling healthier than driving, but it's also one of the best ways to see the sights.

9 Dine early
Seek out dinner deals such as early-bird specials for patrons dining between 5pm and 6pm. Save on restaurant meals and drinks by opting for the set menus.

10 Try street food
Little Havana's Latin American and Cuban restaurants are much less expensive than South Beach.

Festivals

1 South Beach Wine and Food Festival

MAP R4 ■ Feb ■ www.sobewff.org

This popular festival celebrates the talents of renowned wine producers and local and guest chefs.

2 Coconut Grove Arts Festival

3rd Monday in Feb

The Grove is one of the biggest arts festivals (see p110) in the country, complete with all-day concerts, street food, and throngs of arts lovers.

3 Winter Party

MAP R4 ■ Winter Party early Mar ■ www.winterparty.com

This renowned annual LGBTQ+ beach party attracts thousands of visitors from all over the United States. Pumped-up raves go on all night in the choicest South Beach venues.

4 Carnaval Miami

MAP K3 ■ 8th St from 4th–27th aves ■ Early Mar ■ www.carnavalmiami.com

For the Cuban district, March is a time of dancing and singing in the streets to Latin jazz, pop, flamenco, and tango. It culminates on the second Sunday with a large party. Twenty-three blocks of Little Havana are closed off and performers line the way. A fireworks display brings a resounding finale to the festivities.

Miami Film Festival at Miami Dade College

5 Miami Film Festival

Early Mar ■ www.miamifilmfestival.com

Organized by the Film Society of Miami and Miami Dade College (MDC), the Miami Film Festival especially focuses on Ibero-American films. Venues for the event include the Silverspot Cinema in Downtown Miami, Coral Gables Art Cinema, and the Bill Cosford Cinema.

Dressed in colorful costumes, people take to the streets for Carnaval Miami

6 Miami-Dade County Fair and Exposition

MAP E3 ■ Tamiami Park, 10901 Coral Way ■ Mar/Apr ■ www.thefair.me

This traditional American county fair is replete with rides, sideshows, cotton candy, candied apples, live performances, and exhibits relating to farm life and crafts.

7 International Mango Festival

MAP G4 ■ Fairchild Tropical Botanic Gardens ■ Mid-Jul

The luscious fruit is celebrated with gusto – enjoy a complete mango feast.

8 Hispanic Heritage Festival

MAP G3 ■ Throughout Miami-Dade County ■ Sep/Oct

This month-long Latin American celebration has street parties, food festivals, films, music and dance performances, and a fashion show.

Fantasy Fest parade at Key West

9 Fantasy Fest

Mid–Late Oct

For two weeks leading up to Halloween, Key West gives itself over to non-stop celebration (see p127). On the Saturday before the 31st, a parade, featuring floats and costumes, departs from Mallory Square and slowly winds down Duval. Many revelers go nearly-nude, except for a bit of body paint here and a feather or two there.

10 King Mango Strut

Last Sun in Dec

A Coconut Grove spoof on the Orange Bowl Parade (see p110).

TOP 10 MUSIC EVENTS AND FESTIVALS

The Ultra Music Festival in Miami

1 Mile 0 Festival
Late Jan–Feb ■ www.mile0fest.com
The best Red Dirt and Americana musicians come to Key West.

2 Festival of the Arts Boca
Mar ■ www.festivalboca.org
South Florida's classical music festival.

3 Jazz in the Gardens
Mar ■ www.jazzinthegardens.com
Internationally renowned jazz and R&B performances at the Hard Rock Stadium.

4 Winter Music Conference
Mar ■ www.wintermusic conference.com
A week-long electronic music conference, held on Miami Beach.

5 Ultra Music Festival
Late Mar ■ www.ultramusic festival.com
The world's premier electronic music festival takes place in Bayfront Park.

6 Tortuga Music Festival
Apr ■ www.tortugamusicfestival.com
This country, rock, and roots festival funds marine conservation.

7 Afro Roots Festival
Late Apr–May
Live concerts and events across the Keys.

8 Rolling Loud Miami
Jul ■ www.rollingloud.com/miami
Begun in Miami, this three-day event is the world's largest hip-hop festival.

9 Lower Keys Underwater Music Festival
Jul
Unique sub-sea concert held at Looe Key Reef Resort & Dive Center.

10 Ill Points
Oct ■ www.iiipoints.com
The Mana Wynwood Convention Center hosts a music, art, and technology festival.

Walks, Drives, and Cycling Routes

The lush Everglades

spread out around the neighborhood, and most of them are best found by driving, then exploring on foot.

(1) Everglades Trails
There are several roads for exploring the Everglades *(see pp34–5)*: I-75 or Alligator Alley; Highway 41 or the Tamiami Trail; or the less developed road (No. 9336) from Florida City. Off all of these roads, you'll find several opportunities for great excursions into the wild.

(2) Hollywood Broadwalk
Starting some 15 miles (24 km) north of South Beach, the Hollywood Beach Broadwalk *(p47)* runs for 2.5 miles (4 km) along the Atlantic shore. The promenade makes for a pleasant stroll or bike ride as it is lined with stores, local bars, and cafés on one side, and golden sands on the other.

(3) Calle Ocho
The main walkable part of Little Havana *(see pp18–19)* lies along SW 8th Street, between about 11th and 17th avenues. The interesting spots are quite

Paintings of iconic Cubans, Calle Ocho

(4) Coconut Grove
Always lively, usually with a young crowd, this area of Miami *(see pp106–113)* south of Downtown has a great buzz and is ideal for exploring on foot. As well as shops, outdoor restaurants, and cafés, live bands often play in CocoWalk.

(5) Palm Beach
Begin your walk at Worth Avenue on the beach at Ocean Blvd. Stroll west and check out as many of the fabulous shops as you dare. Continue on to Addison Mizner's pink palace, Casa de Leoni (No. 450), then take Lake Drive north to Royal Palm Way. Visit the Society of the Four Arts, then continue north to the Flagler Museum. Finally, go east along Royal Poinciana Way and south to The Breakers *(see p30)*.

(6) Rickenbacker Trail
MAP H3–H4
This 8.5-mile (13-km), paved cycling trail begins south of Downtown Miami and travels the length of Key Biscayne along a dedicated bike lane, taking in ocean views and palm-lined beaches. Starting from Brickell Avenue at Alice Wainwright Park, cycle across the William M. Powell Bridge to Virginia Key, stopping at Hobie Island Beach Park for views of Miami's skyline. Continue across

Bear Cut Bridge to Key Biscayne, passing Crandon Park and ending at Bill Baggs Cape Florida State Park and Lighthouse.

Key West Old Town

The only sensible way to get around Key West (see pp32–3) is either on foot or by bike; there's so much detail to take in and, besides, parking is usually a problem here. A planned tour (see p127) can be fine, but it's just as good to walk wherever inspiration leads.

Art Deco District

With some 800 Tropical Deco wonders to behold, you can hardly miss it; just walk or bike along Ocean Drive, and Collins and Washington avenues between about 5th and 22nd streets (see pp14–17).

The Ocean Drive, Art Deco district

Miami to Key West
MAP D4–A6

There are great sights along this drive, like the giant lobster at the Rain Barrel. Stop to have a seafood meal on the water. Other attractions include parks and nature preserves, such as Bahia Honda State Park (see p121).

⑩ Routes North

If driving north from Miami, take the Gold Coast Highway A1A (see pp30–31) – it makes the time spent worthwhile, rewarding the traveler with both natural beauty and the elegant neighborhoods of the Gold and Treasure Coasts.

TOP 10 ROADSIDE DINERS AND FOOD STOPS

Diners at Mrs. Mac's Kitchen

1 Mrs. Mac's Kitchen, Key Largo
MAP C5 ▪ 99336 Overseas Hwy
No-frills diner famed for its fresh seafood and homemade chili.

2 Ballyhoo's, Key Largo
MAP C5 ▪ 97860 Overseas Hwy
Conch house from the 1930s that features a Friday-night fish fry.

3 Alabama Jack's
MAP D5 ▪ 58000 Card Sound Rd
Tasty conch fritters and live music since the 1950s, on Highway 905A.

4 Hungry Tarpon, Islamorada
MAP C5 ▪ 77522 Overseas Hwy
Scenic views and tuna tacos, cracked conch and Thai-style mahi fish fingers.

5 The Seven Mile Grill, Marathon
MAP B6 ▪ 1240 Overseas Hwy
Well-known for its delicious conch chowder, beer-steamed shrimp, and Key lime pie since 1954.

6 No Name Pub, Big Pine Key
The oldest pub (see p57) in the Keys known for its dollar-bill smothered walls. It serves great thin-crust pizzas.

7 The Village Grill & Pump, Lauderdale-By-The Sea
MAP D3 ▪ 4404 El Mar Dr
Atmospheric place for seafood, steaks and cocktails on Highway A1A.

8 Old Key Lime House, Lantana
MAP D2 ▪ 300 E Ocean Ave
Sublime Key lime pie and seafood in a house dating from 1889.

9 Joanie's Blue Crab Café, Ochopee
An Everglades pit stop (see p137) serving such delicacies as frogs' legs, gator pieces, and Indian fry bread.

10 Robert Is Here, Homestead
This celebrated fruit stand (see p119) always draws a crowd for the smoothies and Key lime milkshakes.

Miami and the Keys Area by Area

An aerial view of Florida Keys, a series of tropical islands

Miami Beach and
  Key Biscayne   **80**

Downtown and Little Havana   **90**

North of Downtown   **98**

Coral Gables and
  Coconut Grove   **106**

South of Coconut Grove   **114**

The Keys   **120**

Side Trips   **132**

📓🔟 Miami Beach and Key Biscayne

Nowhere else on earth seems to be so addicted to glamour as Miami Beach. All the traits of modern life can be seen here, pushed to the limit: symbols of wealth and status are vaunted everywhere you look in this style-conscious part of the city. Key Biscayne, the next big island to the south, provides a contrast to the dynamism of its neighbor; here you will find a tranquil and family-oriented atmosphere pervading parks, perfect beaches, and a scattering of museums.

Cape Florida Light on Key Biscayne

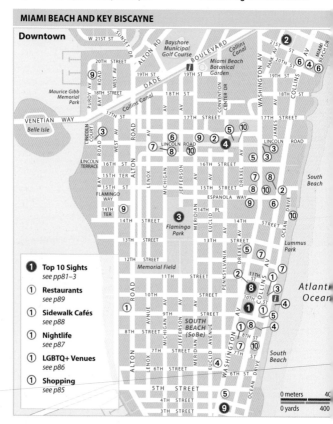

MIAMI BEACH AND KEY BISCAYNE

- **1** Top 10 Sights
  see pp81–3
- **1** Restaurants
  see p89
- **1** Sidewalk Cafés
  see p88
- **1** Nightlife
  see p87
- **1** LGBTQ+ Venues
  see p86
- **1** Shopping
  see p85

The world-famous Art Deco District, at the very heart of South Beach

① SoBe and the Art Deco District

All walks of life meet here in the vibrant community of South Beach, otherwise known as SoBe

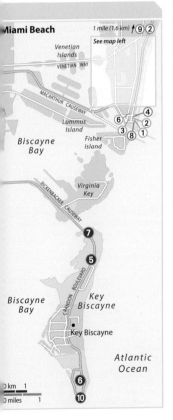

(see pp12–13). Its famous Art Deco District (see pp14–17) is beautifully preserved in hundreds of colorful, Tropical Deco buildings.

② The Bass

MAP S1 ▪ 2100 Collins Ave, South Beach ▪ 305 673 7530 ▪ Open noon–5pm Wed–Sun ▪ Adm ▪ www.thebass.org

This Mayan-influenced Art Deco structure of the 1930s, previously the Miami Beach Public Library and Art Center, came of age in 1964, when John and Johanna Bass donated their extensive collection of art. It consists mainly of 15th–17th-century European paintings, sculpture, and textiles; highlights include Renaissance and Baroque works, as well as paintings by Rubens, and a 16th-century Flemish tapestry.

③ Flamingo Park

MAP R3 ▪ 11th St and Jefferson Ave, South Beach ▪ 305 673 7779 ▪ Open sunrise–10pm daily

This pleasant spot in the heart of South Beach started life in the 1920s as a golf course. Later home to major and minor league baseball teams, the 36-acre- (14-ha-) park has since been extensively renovated. Today the site hosts an array of sports facilities, including baseball and football stadiums, basketball, handball, and tennis courts, and a soccer field. There is also an aquatic center with 2 public pools, and a playground for toddlers.

4 Lincoln Road Mall
MAP R2

Acclaimed as the most glamorous shopping district outside of New York when it debuted in the 1950s, this pedestrianized strip remains lined with hip brand-name stores and cool cafés. Russian-born "Miami Modern" (MiMo) architect Morris Lapidus designed the mall, including its gardens, fountains, and space-age follies that serve as sunshades. Attractions include Oolite Arts (at No. 924), where avant-garde artwork is displayed.

The unique facade of Lincoln Road Mall

5 Crandon Park
MAP H4 ■ 305 365 2320

Key Biscayne is blessed with some of Miami's top beaches. Certainly the most impressive is this one, which is actually rated among the top ten in the country. Located on the upper half of the key, it's 3 miles (5 km) long and enormously wide, with palm trees and picnic areas.

The waters are calm and shallow, and good for snorkeling. Additional bonuses include concession stands, 75 barbecue grills, a pretty winding boardwalk, and convenient parking.

6 Bill Baggs Cape Florida State Park
MAP H4 ■ 786 582 2673 ■ Adm

This beach, also rated among Florida's top ten, is conveniently joined to picnic areas and pavilions by boardwalks across the dunes. The sugary sand is sometimes marred by clumps of seaweed, but it is the stinging Portuguese man-o'-war that you need to watch out for most.

7 Marjory Stoneman Douglas Biscayne Nature Center
MAP H3 ■ 6767 Crandon Blvd, Key Biscayne ■ 9am–3pm daily ■ www.biscaynenaturecenter.org

Overlooking the ocean at the north end of Crandon Park, this center contains a unique black mangrove reef of fossilized wood and roots. It is possible to wade in shallow waters to explore the underwater world with suitable foot protection on. The nature center is named after the woman who almost single-handedly saved the Everglades from being overrun by housing developments, and it offers information and guided tours.

Beautiful Crandon Park Beach

Visitors at The Wolfsonian–FIU

8 The Wolfsonian–FIU

A museum and design research institute *(see pp28–9)* that traces the origins of Deco and other significant modern artistic trends.

9 Jewish Museum of Florida

MAP R5 ▪ 301 Washington Ave, South Beach ▪ 305 672 5044 ▪ Open 10am–4pm Wed–Sun ▪ www.jmof.fiu.edu

This fascinating museum chronicles the Jewish experience in Florida, with more than 100,000 items in the permanent collection. Highlights include a rare porcelain plate from 1865, an ornate ivory-covered Confirmation Bible printed in Vienna in 1911, and 19th-century community wedding rings from central Europe.

10 Cape Florida Light

MAP H4 ▪ Tours at 10am & 1pm Thu–Mon; 109 steps to the top

The oldest structure in South Florida has been standing sentinel since 1825. In 1836, it was destroyed by Native Americans, only to be reborn ten years later. It has since withstood meteorological onslaughts, and in 1966 its renovation and preservation began.

MIAMI VICE

September 16, 1984, was a day that altered Miami overnight. It was the day *Miami Vice* debuted on TV, setting the stage for the city to conquer the world of high-profile glitz and hedonism. Suddenly the slick, candy-colored world of edgy outlaws, fast cars, and deals caught the global imagination, and Miami was the place to be.

A WALK THROUGH THE ART DECO DISTRICT

Abbey Hotel
SLS South Beach
Delano
Loews Miami Beach
Collins Avenue
FL Café
Cardozo
Carlyle
Leslie
Clevelander
Ocean Drive
from 6th Street
1 mile (1.6 km)

▶ MORNING

From the southern end of the District on **Ocean Drive** *(see p13)*, at 6th Street, head northward, checking out not just the facades but also as many of the hotel interiors as you can. Many have unique design elements in the lobbies, bars, and gardens. Between the **Leslie** *(see p15)* and the **Cardozo** *(see p14)* is the wonderful Carlyle, now operating as a condominium. Turn left at 13th Street and walk to Collins Avenue. Turn right on Collins and stop for lunch at **FL Café** *(No. 1360 at 14th Street)*, set in an historic Art Deco building that dates to 1934.

AFTERNOON

A little farther on, you'll find the **Loews Miami Beach** *(see p148)*, which features a cut coral facade and neon lights. At No. 1685, admire the all-white **Delano** *(see p149)*, with its landmark winged tower. The outlandish Postmodern interiors were by Philippe Starck, and contain original Dali and Gaudi furniture. Next stop is the SLS South Beach, with another fantasy glass tower block. When you get to 21st Street, turn left; on the next corner you will encounter the Abbey Hotel, with its marvelous salamander motif and Flash Gordon-style towers. Retrace your steps and cap the walk with a drink at the **Clevelander** *(see p88)*, a beautiful spot to end your day in the Art Deco District.

See map on pp80–81

Sports Options

① Swimming

The hotel pool or the blue Atlantic Ocean? This is Florida, and swimming is number one – snorkeling, too, in quieter areas, especially Crandon Park on Key Biscayne (see p82) and South Pointe.

Windsurfers catching the wind

② Surfing and Windsurfing

Miami Water Sports: www. miamiwatersports.com

For windsurfing in the area, the intracoastal waterways are calm and breezy; check out Miami Water Sports for rentals. The Atlantic side offers great conditions for surfing; the best spot is just off South Pointe Beach.

③ Cycling

Miami Beach Bicycle Center: bikemiamibeach.com

Cycling is the best way to get around both Miami Beach and Key Biscayne.

④ Jet-Skiing

Rentals are available at Hobie Island Beach and on the beaches at Virginia Key (see p50); weave through the waves and head for the horizon.

⑤ Workouts

South Pointe Park has a famous calisthenics circuit you can huff and puff your way through while taking in the views of Miami Beach.

⑥ Volleyball

Anywhere there's a developed beach you're likely to find a volleyball net and a quorum of players. Lummus Park is the best place to show off your skills to Miami's greatest beach bums, but South Pointe Park's a close contender.

⑦ Tennis

Miami-Dade County Parks and Recreation Department: www.miami dade.gov ■ Flamingo Park Tennis Center: www.miamibeachfl.gov

There are plenty of tennis courts available for rental all over the area.

⑧ Golf

MAP H4 ■ Crandon Golf at Key Biscayne: 6700 Crandon Blvd; 305 361 9129; https://golfcrandon.com

The main reason that Jackie Gleason (see p61) moved to Miami is so that he could play golf year-round. The Crandon golf course on Key Biscayne is one of the best.

⑨ Kite-Flying

This is a very popular activity, given the prevailing maritime winds. There's even a park especially for kite enthusiasts, which is located at the south end of Haulover Park.

⑩ Fishing

Deep-sea fishing out in the ocean, or the more conventional kind off a jetty or pier – both are readily available. The jetty or South Pointe Park Pier on Miami Beach is good, or the breaker area just south of the Lighthouse on Key Biscayne.

Anglers on the pier, Sunny Isles Beach

Shopping

(1) Collins Avenue from 6th to 9th Streets, South Beach
MAP R4

This area has designer boutiques in ample supply including Armani Exchange, Dolce Vita, Rip Curl, and Free People. Also present are mall favorites such as Sunglass Hut, Shoe Palace, and Vans.

(2) Runway Swimwear
MAP R2 ▪ 609 Lincoln Rd, Miami Beach

Prepare for the beach by picking up the latest swimwear fashions for men and women here.

(3) Bachi Jewels
MAP S3 ▪ 1627 Washington Ave, Miami Beach

Popular with Miami Beach locals, this jewelry store stocks everything from cheap faux turquoise chains to custom-made diamond rings. It also offers repairs.

(4) Art Deco Welcome Center

Besides a wealth of information about this historic district (see p15), you'll discover a treasure trove of Deco kitsch to take home as your very own. There's everything from cutesy salt and pepper sets to really rather nice reproduction lamps.

(5) Lids
MAP R2 ▪ 521 Lincoln Rd, Miami Beach

With a large selection of sport apparel, fashion wear, and collegiate hats, Lids is the ideal place to purchase gifts that won't take up much room in your suitcase.

(6) Original Penguin
MAP R2 ▪ 925 Lincoln Rd, Miami Beach

With its trademark loud prints and menswear, this iconic American sportswear brand is especially popular in Miami Beach.

The lavish interiors of The Webster

(7) The Webster
MAP S3 ▪ 1220 Collins Ave, Miami Beach ▪ 305 674 7899

Men's and women's fashions from top designers are available here. There's even a restaurant, Caviar Kaspia, where you can buy gourmet gift baskets to take home.

(8) Beach Bunny Swimwear
MAP Q2 ▪ 1006 Lincoln Rd, Miami Beach

Shop for ladies' swimwear, beach clothing, and sunny accessories, including hats, sandals, and even designer towels.

(9) P448 Miami Beach
MAP R3 ▪ 420 Espanola Way, Miami Beach ▪ 305 763 8466

Funky Italian footwear brand with street shoes and colorful sneakers. The store itself is worth a look inside for street art and colorful murals by local artists.

(10) Ban de Osh
MAP R2 ▪ 816 Lincoln Rd, Miami Beach ▪ 768 708 5757 ▪ www.bandeosh.com

Mediterranean-inspired slow fashion store selling women's clothing, swimwear, and home accessories. Everything has a breezy, boho-chic vibe befitting of Miami Beach. This is a perfect place to pick up festival wear or a unique piece of funky jewelry to take home.

See map on pp80–81

LGBTQ+ Venues

Outdoor seating at the Palace Bar

1 Palace Bar
MAP S3 ■ 1052 Ocean Dr, South Beach ■ 305 531 7234 ■ www.palacesouthbeach.com

The first LGBTQ+ restaurant and bar on Ocean Drive, in the heart of the Art Deco District. Popular for weekend drag shows, and varied menus.

2 Twist
MAP R4 ■ 1057 Washington Ave, South Beach ■ 305 538 9478 ■ www.twistsobe.com

SoBe's largest LGBTQ+ venue, with seven bars in one, has something on every night. Happy hour 3–9pm daily.

3 Bar at Hotel Gaythering
MAP Q2 ■ 1409 Lincoln Rd, South Beach ■ www.gaythering.com

A congenial lounge bar with a laid-back atmosphere, where soft ambient music does not overpower conversation. It specializes in micro beers and craft cocktails. Large HD TVs play shows and sporting events.

4 Big Pink
MAP R5 ■ 157 Collins Ave, Miami Beach ■ 305 532 4700

This somewhat kitschy, retro diner-themed haunt is hard to miss thanks to the pink VW Beetles parked outside. The lengthy menu of comfort foods contains more than 200 items, and portions are huge.

5 Nathan's Bar
MAP R4 ■ 1216 Washington Ave, Miami Beach ■ www.nathans-bar.com

Owned by a former Twist mixologist, this bar with a retro decor was started in 2021. It features superb drag acts and serves a variety of cocktails.

6 Kill Your Idol
MAP S3 ■ 222 Española Way, South Beach ■ 305 534 1009

A statue of Bruce Lee hovers above the bar, and the Monday drag shows attract the biggest LGBTQ+ contingent.

7 12th Street Beach
Marked by fluttering rainbow-colored flags, this is SoBe's "semi-official" LGBTQ+ beach. It's located right in the middle of Lummus Park, the venue for Pride Festival and Winter Party.

8 Axelbeach Miami
MAP ■ 1500 Collins Ave, Miami Beach ■ www.axelhotels.com

This gay-friendly hotel chain has opened a branch only a few steps away from Miami Beach. The wonderful Tropical Deco interior is pure modern Miami.

9 Spris
MAP R2 ■ 731 Lincoln Rd, Miami Beach ■ 305 673 2020

Popular people-watching spot named after the famous aperitif from the Veneto. Eclectic menu of gourmet pizza and shareable plates.

10 The Betsy Hotel
MAP S3 ■ 1440 Ocean Dr, Miami Beach ■ www.thebetsyhotel.com

A beachfront boutique hotel that bills itself as a "community artistic oasis" and supports LGBTQ+ arts and events.

VW Beetle, parked outside Big Pink

Nightlife

(1) Voodoo
MAP S4 ▪ 928 Ocean Dr,
Miami Beach ▪ 305 206 6404
▪ www.voodoo.miami

A lively club, Voodoo serves a wide range of drinks. It features decent house DJs, and is crowned by the Voodoo Rooftop & Hookah Lounge.

(2) Basement
MAP S1 ▪ 2901 Collins Ave,
Miami Beach ▪ www.basement
miami.com

It is never a boring night at this buzzing nightclub founded by the legendary owner of Studio 54. The venue is popular with Miami's glitterati, who come here to dance, bowl, or skate at its mini ice skating rink.

(3) MR JONES
MAP S2 ▪ 320
Lincoln Rd, Miami Beach
▪ 305 602 3117 ▪ www.
mrjonesmiami.com

This late-night restaurant and club stays lively until 5am. It features hip-hop music.

(4) Mynt
MAP S2 ▪ 1921 Collins
Ave, Miami Beach ▪ 305 532
0727 ▪ www.myntlounge.com

Sample a tipple or two from the cocktail menu at this stylish nightspot that is frequented by a hip South Beach crowd.

(5) Do Not Sit on the Furniture
MAP R3 ▪ 423 16th St, Miami Beach,
▪ 510 551 5067 ▪ www.donotsitonthe
furniture.com

Specializing in underground dance music, this popular club hosts well-known local and international DJs.

(6) Watr at the 1 Rooftop
MAP S1 ▪ 1 Hotel, 2341
Collins Ave, Miami Beach ▪ 305
604 1000 ▪ www.1hotels.com

Featuring a rooftop bar with ocean views and an eco-chic aesthetic, Watr serves cocktails made with sustainable ingredients. Reservations are required for non-hotel guests.

(7) Exchange Miami
MAP H2 ▪ 1532 Washington
Ave, Miami Beach ▪ 305 763 8264
▪ www.exchangemia.com

This luxurious club has a decent roster of resident and celebrity guest DJs.

(8) Nikki Beach Miami
MAP R5 ▪ 1 Ocean Dr, South
Beach ▪ 305 538 1111 ▪ www.miami-beach.nikkibeach.com

There are several bars and dance floors here; downstairs is the up-beat Nikki Beach, and upstairs the exclusive Club 01.

Partying on the dance floor at LIV

(9) LIV
MAP H3 ▪ 4441 Collins Ave,
Miami Beach ▪ 305 674 4680
▪ www.livnightclub.com

Located in the Fontainebleau Miami Beach, LIV is a massive, high-energy and exclusive dance club.

(10) Treehouse
MAP S1 ▪ 323 23rd St,
Miami Beach ▪ 786 318 1908
▪ www.treehousemiami.com

This nightclub features a lineup of international DJs. Its neon-lit dance floor hosts house and techno raves. There's an outdoor seating area to enjoy, too.

See map on pp80–81

Sidewalk Cafés

1 Taste Bakery Cafe
MAP Q4 ▪ 900 Alton Rd, Miami Beach ▪ www.taste-bakery.com ▪ $$

Enjoy all-day breakfasts, salads, and sandwiches, with fresh juice, smoothies, or roasted coffee at this popular neighborhood bakery and café.

2 Front Porch Café
MAP S3 ▪ 1458 Ocean Dr, Miami Beach ▪ 305 531 8300 ▪ $$

A popular South Beach breakfast and lunch spot, Front Porch also attracts smart crowds for dinner and during happy hours on its outdoor terrace.

3 Clevelander
MAP S4 ▪ 1020 Ocean Dr, South Beach ▪ $$

Facing the beach on the sidewalk, this always has something going on: listen to the live music, have something to eat, or just relax.

4 Pelican Café
MAP S4 ▪ 826 Ocean Dr, South Beach ▪ $$

Grab a seat on the outdoor patio and sample dishes such as fresh pastas and Mediterranean salads. There's also a choice breakfast menu.

5 Mango's Tropical Café
MAP S4 ▪ 900 Ocean Dr, at 9th St ▪ $

Always hot, with a huge Floribbean menu. The action spills outside.

Alfresco dining, Mango's Tropical Café

6 The Ocean Grill
MAP S2 ▪ 2001 Collins Ave, Miami Beach ▪ 855 923 7899 ▪ www.thesetaihotels.com ▪ $$

This beachfront restaurant serves artfully prepared southern European, American, as well as seafood classics cooked on a wood-fired grill.

7 Segafredo L'Originale
MAP R2 ▪ 1040 Lincoln Rd, Miami Beach ▪ www.sze-originale.com ▪ $

This stylish Italian café turns into a hip bar at night. During the day, it offers tasty gelato, espresso, iced coffee, and Italian soft drinks such as Chinotto.

8 Panther Coffee – Miami Beach
MAP Q2 ▪ 1875 Purdy Ave, Miami Beach ▪ www.panthercoffee.com ▪ $

Miami's famous artisanal coffee producer roasts its beans in Wynwood and Little Haiti. A range of espresso drinks and pastries are on offer.

9 Cantina Beach
MAP H4 ▪ 455 Grand Bay Dr, Key Biscayne ▪ 305 365 4500 ▪ $$

Dine on slow-braised chicken enchiladas at this oceanfront Mexican restaurant in the Ritz-Carlton.

10 Wet Willie's
MAP S4 ▪ 760 Ocean Dr, South Beach ▪ $$

This bar attracts a young, post-beach crowd with its powerful frozen drinks with names such as Call-A-Cab.

Restaurants

1 **The Local House**
MAP R5 ▪ 400 Ocean Dr, Miami Beach ▪ 786 230 8396 ▪ www. localhouse.com ▪ $$
Order lobster mac & cheese or try the tofu poke bowl at this hidden gem, a block from the beach.

Entrance of The Local House restaurant

2 **Prime 112**
MAP R5 ▪ 112 Ocean Dr, Miami Beach ▪ 305 532 8112 ▪ $$$
The South Beach elite tuck into juicy steaks and excellent seafood served by waiters in butcher-stripe aprons.

3 **Joe's Stone Crab**
MAP R5 ▪ 11 Washington Ave, South Beach ▪ 305 673 0365 ▪ $$
Expect gloriously sweet stone crabs and a notorious wait to get in. Also try Miami's best Key lime pie.

Crab dish, Joe's Stone Crab

4 **Queen Miami Beach**
MAP R4 ▪ 550 Washington Ave, Miami Beach ▪ 786 373 2930 ▪ www. queenmiamibeach.com ▪ $$$
This Japanese restaurant, set inside the old Paris Theater, has a raw bar and serves great sushi and top-grade beef cuts sourced from small farms.

5 **Fratelli la Bufala**
MAP R5 ▪ 437 Washington Ave, Miami Beach ▪ 305 532 0700 ▪ $$
The best pizza in town is served at this South Beach Italian spot, cooked in a wood-burning stove.

PRICE CATEGORIES
For a three-course meal for one with half a bottle of wine (or equivalent meal), taxes, and extra charges.

$ under $35 $$ $35–$70 $$$ over $70

6 **Stubborn Seed**
MAP R5 ▪ 101 Washington Ave, Miami Beach ▪ www.stubbornseed. com ▪ $$$
Owned by Jeremy Ford, one of the winners of *Top Chef* (see p66) offers an eight-course menu, tasty desserts, and cocktails.

7 **Puerto Sagua Restaurant**
MAP R4 ▪ 700 Collins Ave, Miami Beach ▪ 305 673 1115 ▪ $
Traditional Cuban fare is what brings queues out the door here. Regulars swear by the *ropa vieja* and oxtail.

8 **Pane & Vino**
MAP S2 ▪ 1450 Washington Ave, South Beach ▪ 305 535 9027 ▪ $$
Cozy Italian restaurant from Sicilian chef GianPaolo Ferrera, featuring candlelit tables, elegant decor, and tasty dishes with homemade pasta. Be sure to try Paolo's celebrated Cannolo Siciliano for dessert.

9 **Barton G – The Restaurant**
MAP Q3 ▪ 1427 West Ave, Miami Beach ▪ 305 672 8881 ▪ $$$
Popular with locals, Barton G serves American comfort food with a twist. The lush orchid garden is a great setting for a romantic meal.

10 **Yuca 105**
MAP R2 ▪ 501 Lincoln Rd, Miami Beach ▪ 786 577 3500 ▪ $$
The name Yuca stands for Young Urban Cuban Americans. South Florida's original upscale Cuban restaurant has Nuevo Latino cuisine, trendy decor, and live entertainment.

See map on pp80–81

TOP 10 Downtown and Little Havana

For many visitors, this part of Miami is the most fascinating. Here along the Miami River is where it all started in the late 1800s, but it took the arrival of Cuban exiles from the 1950s on for Miami to come into its own. On these busy streets, the Cuban community still thrives in the south, and Latin American influence in Miami continues to grow.

① Freedom Tower
MAP N1 ■ 600 Biscayne Blvd, Downtown ■ Open 1–6pm Wed & Fri–Sun (to 8pm Thu) ■ Adm ■ www.moadmdc.org

Built in 1925 in the Mediterranean Revival style, this Downtown landmark was inspired by the 800-year-old bell tower of Seville Cathedral. Once home to the now-defunct *Miami Daily News*, and in the 1960s a reception center to process Cubans fleeing Castro, the building was restored in 1988 to create a Cuban museum. Today it holds the MDC Museum of Art + Design.

The iconic Freedom Tower

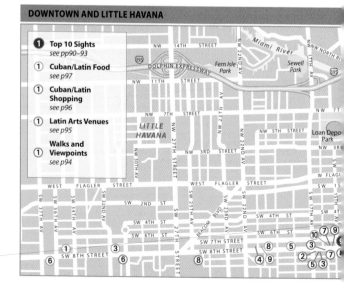

DOWNTOWN AND LITTLE HAVANA

- ❶ Top 10 Sights
  see pp90–93
- ① Cuban/Latin Food
  see p97
- ① Cuban/Latin Shopping
  see p96
- ① Latin Arts Venues
  see p95
- ① Walks and Viewpoints
  see p94

2 David W. Dyer Federal Building

MAP N1 ■ 300 North Miami Ave, Downtown ■ Open 8:30am–4:30pm Mon–Fri, closed during major trials

An imposing Neo-Classical edifice, finished in 1931, it has since hosted high-profile trials, including that of Manuel Noriega, the former president of Panama, in 1990. The second-floor mural entitled *Law Guides Florida's Progress* is designed by Denman Fink, famous for his work in Coral Gables. It depicts Florida's evolution from a tropical backwater to one of America's most prosperous states.

Exhibit at Frost Museum of Science

3 Pérez Art Museum

MAP G3 ■ 1103 Biscayne Blvd, Downtown ■ 305 375 3000 ■ Open 11am–6pm Fri–Mon (to 9pm Thu) ■ Adm ■ www.pamm.org

Set in lush gardens, this art museum, showcases international and contemporary work. Designed by architects Herzog & de Meuron, its galleries feature temporary exhibitions in various mediums and a permanent collection including contemporary Cuban art donated to the museum by its well known benefactor, Jorge M. Pérez.

4 Phillip and Patricia Frost Museum of Science

MAP G3 ■ 1101 Biscayne Blvd, Downtown ■ 305 434 9600 ■ Open 10am–6pm daily ■ www.frost science.org

This museum relocated to new digs in 2017 (Miami entrepreneur Phillip Frost donated $35 million to the site). The campus features an aquarium, a planetarium, and the North and West Wings. The latter host interactive exhibits covering an exploration of the Everglades, the human body and mind, the story of flight, and the latest innovations in technology.

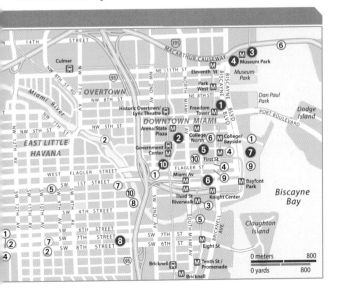

Bayside Marketplace running alongside the waterfront

5 Gesu Church

MAP N1 ■ 118 NE 2nd St, Downtown ■ 305 379 1424

This Mediterranean Revival building in the Spanish Colonial style (built in 1922) is the oldest Catholic church in Miami. The church is noted for its stained-glass windows and the ceiling mural restored by a lone Nicaraguan refugee in the late 1980s.

Detail inside the Gesu Church

6 Miami Tower

MAP N2 ■ International Place, 100 SE 2nd St, Downtown

Built in 1983, this striking skyscraper is the work of architect I. M. Pei, famous for the glass pyramid in the courtyard of the Louvre in Paris. This building is notable both during the day for its Op-Art horizontal banding across the stepped hemi-cylinders, and at night for the changing colors of its overall illumination.

7 Bayside Marketplace and Bayfront Park

MAP P1–P2 ■ 401 Biscayne Blvd at 4th St, Downtown ■ Open 10am–10pm Mon–Thu (to 11pm Fri & Sat), 11am–9pm Sun ■ www.bayside marketplace.com

Curving around Miamarina, this shopping and entertainment complex is undeniably fun and the Downtown area's best attraction. It's not South Beach, but La Vida Loca echoes here, too, often with live salsa bands playing on the esplanade. Shops – including Express, Victoria's Secret, Sketchers, and Foot Locker – and 30 restaurants, with everything from ice cream to paella, make it a happening place. To the south, Bayfront Park, designed by Isamu Noguchi, is extensive and can provide a pleasant interlude of greenery, water, monuments, sculpture, and striking views.

GATEWAY TO LATIN AMERICA

Two-thirds of Miami's population is of Hispanic origin. Pick up the *Miami Herald* and you'll see that the news of the day in Caracas, Bogotá, Managua, and – above all – Havana is given top billing. All these connections, for good or ill, have made Miami the US kingpin when it comes to dealing with Latin and South America.

8 Calle Ocho and Around

This area is a slice of Cuban culture, liberally spiced up with all sorts of other Hispanic and Caribbean influences. Since Castro's Communist revolution in Cuba, Miami has become the main destination for wave after wave of immigrants fleeing the island that some still long for as home (see pp18–19).

9 Cubaocho Museum

MAP J3 ■ 1465 SW 8th St, Little Havana ■ 305 285 5880 ■ Open 10am–midnight Mon–Fri, 11am–3am Sat & Sun ■ www.cubaocho.com

The rich legacy of Cuban Americans is celebrated at this cultural center established by collector Roberto Ramos, who escaped Cuba by boat in 1992. The main gallery displays a collection of pre-revolutionary artwork (1800 to the 1960s), including the massive 1937 painting "La Rumba" by Antonio Sánchez Araujo.

10 Miami-Dade Cultural Center

MAP M2 ■ 101 W Flagler St, Downtown ■ Library: open 10am–6pm Mon–Sat

Designed by the celebrated American architect Philip Johnson in 1982, the Mediterranean-style complex, set around a tiled plaza, incorporates the informative, interactive HistoryMiami (see p43) and the Main Public Library, which contains four million books.

Miami-Dade Cultural Center

A TRIP THROUGH CALLE OCHO

▶ MID-MORNING

First stop, if you like a cigar, is the **Little Havana Cigar Factory** (see p19) on SW 11th Ave. Just across SW 15th Ave you will find the **Cubaocho Museum**. Soak up the exuberant collection of Cuban art here, perhaps grabbing a coffee at the café inside. Come back later that evening to catch live performances and enjoy an expertly made mojito at the bar. Next stop is SW 13th Avenue, to see the monuments to fallen Cuban freedom fighters at the **Brigade 2506 Memorial** Eternal Flame (see p18), before a sortie into the delightful fruit market at No. 1334, **Los Pinareños Fruteria** (see p96). At the corner of SW 15th Ave, peek in on **Domino Park** (see p18) where there's always at least one game going on. Then take time to stop for coffee and maybe a snack at the wonderful **La Colada**, at No. 1518. The "house of Cuban coffee" uses organic Cuban coffee beans.

LATE MORNING

Continuing on to the next block, at No. 1652, take in the exciting Latin American art displayed at the **Taberna del Pintor Agustín Gaínza** (see p96), where you're likely to meet the affable artist himself. After that, try a free-form ramble of discovery – but don't miss the gaudy entrance to **La Casa de los Trucos** (see p96), at No. 1343. When it's time for lunch, head for **La Carreta I** (see p97), on the south side of Calle Ocho. Enjoy good Cuban food at reasonable prices in this family restaurant.

See map on pp90–91 ←

Walks and Viewpoints

 Bayside Marketplace
Adjacent to the impressive Miami-Dade Arena, this complex (see p92) feels part Disney theme-park, part international bazaar. Located right on the waterfront, it's always good for a stroll.

Fun merchandise for sale, Calle Ocho

 Calle Ocho Walk
Check out the shops and sample various Cuban delicacies between 11th and 17th avenues (see pp18–19).

 Miami Riverwalk
MAP N2
This riverside promenade runs along the north bank of the Miami River and passes around the skyscrapers from Bayfront Park to the South West 2nd Street bridge.

④ **Architectural Walk**
MAP N1–N2
The buildings highlighted on pages 90–93 are lined up over about six blocks along NE–SE 1st and 2nd avenues. Another building worth a look is the Neo-Classical Revival Miami-Dade County Courthouse, three blocks away. Don't miss the ceiling mosaics in the lobby.

 A Ride on the Metromover
The free Metromover (see p141) consists of two elevated loops running around Downtown, so it's a great way to get an over-view of the area.

 Views of Downtown
MAP Q5 & M6
Some of the best views of Downtown are afforded from the freeways. Coming across MacArthur Causeway from South Beach, you'll get some dazzling perspectives, especially at night. The finest view of the skyline is from the Rickenbacker Causeway.

⑦ **A Calle Ocho Café**
El Rey De Las Fritas (see p97) is a wonderful place to sample Cuban food and watch the fasci-nating street life all around.

 A Stroll in José Martí Park
MAP M2
This charming little park by the Miami River is graced with colonnades and pavilions, Spanish-style clusters of street lamps, palm trees, and an excellent children's playground.

⑨ **A Stroll in Bayfront Park**
MAP P1–P2
Right on beautiful Biscayne Bay, this park was designed by Isamu Noguchi "as a wedge of art in the heart of the New World." Here, in addition to Noguchi's sculptures you will find lush greenery, a small sand beach, tropical rock garden, cascading fountain, palms, and olive trees.

⑩ **A Trip Through Little Havana**
To get the overall feel and extent of Little Havana (see pp18–19), head from José Martí Park in the west to 34th Avenue in the east, where you can find the Woodlawn Park North Cemetery and Versailles Restaurant.

Cubaocho Museum, Little Havana

Latin Arts Venues

The intriguing east facade of the Pérez Art Museum Miami

1 Pérez Art Museum Miami
This museum *(see p91)* has a permanent collection of Cuban art. Look out for works by Wisredo Lamb, a modern Cuban artist, who is represented in this section.

2 Latin Art Core
MAP J3 ▪ 1646 SW 8th St ▪ www.latinartcore.com
This Calle Ocho art gallery showcases fine art, including paintings and sculptures, by noted Latin American and Cuban artists, such as Ramon Alejandro and Perez Crespo.

3 Taberna del Pintor Agustín Gaínza
MAP J3 ▪ 1652 SW 8th St ▪ 305 644 5855 ▪ www.agustingainza.com
Admire the work of Cuban-born Agustín Gaínza, whose *oeuvre* covers every medium including painting, print-making, ceramics, and recycled bottles.

4 Teatro 8
MAP G3 ▪ 2173 SW 8th St ▪ www.teatro8.com
Home to the Hispanic Theater Guild. Its directors try to choose topical plays that will become a force for renewal in the Cuban community.

5 Manuel Artime Theater
MAP L2 ▪ 900 SW 1st St ▪ www.miamigov.com/manuelartime
A former Baptist church has been converted into an 800-seat theater. It's home to the Miami Hispanic Ballet.

6 MDC Live Arts
MAP N1 ▪ Miami-Dade Community College, Wolfson Campus 300 NE 2nd Ave, at NE 3rd St ▪ www.liveartsmiami.org
The Performance Series presents music, dance, film, and visual arts.

7 Miami Hispanic Cultural Art Center
MAP L2 ▪ 111 Southwest 5th Ave ▪ 786 278 0474 ▪ www.miamihispanic culturalartscenter.org
The Miami Hispanic Ballet Company, Cuban Classical Ballet of Miami, and Creation Art Center are based here.

8 Casa Juancho
MAP G3 ▪ 2436 SW 8th Ave ▪ 305 642 2452 ▪ www.casa juancho.com
This restaurant presents award-winning cuisine, as well as Spanish performances and a flamenco show.

9 Olympia Theater
MAP N2 ▪ 174 E Flagler St ▪ www.olympiatheater.org
This place features Latin American performances including films during the annual Miami Film Festival.

10 Old's Havana
MAP J3 ▪ 1442 SW 8th St ▪ www.oldshavana.com
This lively Cuban bar and kitchen pays tribute to vintage Havana and hosts regular live entertainment.

See map on pp90–91 ←

Cuban/Latin Shopping

1 La Casa de los Trucos
MAP K3 ▪ 1343 SW 8th St
▪ 305 858 5029

This is the place to come for all your costuming needs. Featuring the most predictable and the most bizarre, this shop has a vast inventory to buy or rent, and excellent prices.

2 Botánica La Negra Francisca
MAP K3 ▪ 1323 SW 8th St

The most atmospheric of the *botánicas* along the main section of Calle Ocho.

3 Little Havana Visitor Center
MAP J3 ▪ 1600 SW 8th St, Miami
▪ 305 643 5500

A unique gift shop and gallery selling Cuban souvenirs and apparel, Little Havana Visitor Center is also home to the only Coca-Cola memorabilia shop in all of Miami.

4 Los Pinareños Fruteria
MAP K3 ▪ 1334 SW 8th St

A delightful fruit market with all sorts of Caribbean produce, such as mamey and small "apple" bananas.

5 Taberna del Pintor
The gallery *(see p95)* is named after the celebrated Cuban artist whose work is on display here along with that of other contemporary Cuban and Latin American artists.

Artifacts for sale at Sentir Cubano

6 Sentir Cubano
MAP G3 ▪ 3100 SW 8th St
▪ 305 644 8870 ▪ www.sentir cubano.com

Look for the vivid murals painted on the side of the building and you'll know you've arrived at this crazy store loaded with Cuban memorabilia.

7 Versailles Bakery
MAP G3 ▪ 3501 SW 8th St
▪ 305 441 2500

Delicious homemade pastries will satisfy your sweet tooth, plus desserts like flan and cheesecake accompanied by Cuban coffee.

8 Little Havana Gift Shop
MAP J3 ▪ 1522 SW 8th St

This little shop has a wide range of Cuban-themed souvenirs on display including T-shirts, hats, wooden sculptures, and paintings.

9 Little Havana Cigar Factory
Enjoy the finest cigars money can buy *(see p19)*. Expert staff are happy to make person- alized recommendations.

10 Seybold Building
MAP N2 ▪ 36 NE 1st St
▪ 305 374 7922

This building has several floors of jewelry and watches as well as wholesale and retail stores. The prices are good value and with so many choices, you will have a hard time deciding what to buy.

Artwork at Taberna del Pintor

Cuban/Latin Food

PRICE CATEGORIES
For a three-course meal for one with half a bottle of wine (or equivalent meal), taxes, and extra charges.

$ under $35 $$ $35–$70 $$$ over $70

1 Versailles Restaurant
MAP G3 ▪ 3555 SW 8th St, at SW 35th Ave ▪ 305 444 0240 ▪ $$

A Little Havana institution, Versailles *(see p67)* is actually a Cuban diner in a very sleek guise.

2 Garcia's Seafood Grille & Fish Market
MAP L1 ▪ 398 NW North River Dr ▪ 305 375 0765 ▪ $$

A family-run restaurant with a friendly atmosphere, though you might have a bit of a wait. Great grouper chowder and conch steak.

3 El Atlacatl
MAP G3 ▪ 3199 SW 8th St ▪ 305 649 8000 ▪ $$

The cuisine of El Salvador, served in a spacious, cheerful setting. Pleasant murals, and a menu that leans toward chicken and seafood.

4 CVI.CHE 105
MAP P1 ▪ 105 NE 3rd Ave ▪ www.ceviche105.com ▪ $$

Chic Peruvian restaurant displaying eclectic artwork, and helmed by Juan Chipoco, who is well-known for his tasty, fresh, and zesty ceviches.

5 El Rey De Las Fritas
MAP J3 ▪ 1821 SW 8th St ▪ 305 644 6054 ▪ $

No-frills Cuban diner *(see p66)* specializing in Cuban-style burgers known as *fritas* (ground beef patty with sautéed onions, thinly sliced fried potatoes and a special sauce).

6 La Carreta
MAP G3 ▪ 3632 SW 8th St ▪ 305 444 7501 ▪ $

From the food to the clientele, this family restaurant in the heart of Little Havana is thoroughly Cuban. Good food at reasonable prices ensures its popularity. Open until late at night.

7 Café la Trova
MAP K3 ▪ 971 SW 8th St ▪ 786 615 4379 ▪ $$

Enjoy Cuban-style dishes from chef Michelle Bernstein at this café, alongside delectable artisanal, handcrafted cocktails. Live music provides enterainment.

8 Guayacan
MAP J3 ▪ 1933 SW 8th St ▪ 305 649 2015 ▪ $$

Cozy and unpretentious, this is Cuban fare with a Nicaraguan twist. Try the *pescado a la Tipitapa*, a whole red snapper deep-fried and drenched in a sauce of onions and peppers.

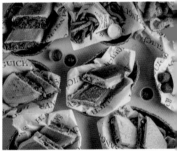
Scrumptious bites at Sanguich

9 Sanguich
MAP G3 ▪ 2057 SW 8th St ▪ 305 539 0969 ▪ $

This splendid sandwich shop, which is decorated in colorful ceramic tiles, marble countertops, and elegant brass trimmings serves delicious Cuban classics at great prices.

10 El Cristo
MAP J3 ▪ 1543 SW 8th ▪ 305 643 9992 ▪ $

This old-fashioned restaurant set in the heart of Little Havana serves up classic Cuban dishes such as *ropa vieja* and *arroz con pollo*.

See map on pp90–91 ←

TOP 10 North of Downtown

The areas north of Miami Beach and Downtown are an irreconcilable juxtaposition of urban sprawl and chic, with acutely deprived areas right alongside the playground of a wealthy elite. Although the beaches are among the city's greatest (and quietest), little else in

the area is well known, and it receives few visitors. Nevertheless, there are local delights to be discovered here. Some of Greater Miami's most fascinating historic sights, including one of the oldest buildings in the Americas, a thriving arts scene, and a range of fine dining options are all well worth seeking out.

Mural by Serge Toussaint in Little Haiti

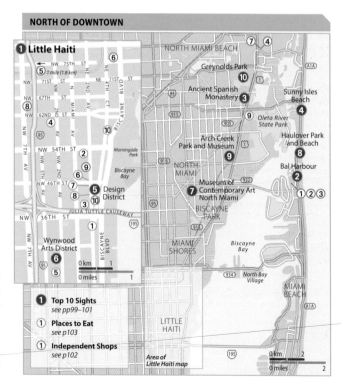

NORTH OF DOWNTOWN

① **Little Haiti**

Morningside Park

Biscayne Bay

Design District

Wynwood Arts District

0 km 1
0 miles 1

NORTH MIAMI BEACH

Greynolds Park ⑩

Ancient Spanish Monastery ③

Sunny Isles Beach ④

Oleta River State Park ⑨

Arch Creek Park and Museum ⑨

NORTH MIAMI

Haulover Park and Beach ⑧

Bal Harbour ②

Museum of Contemporary Art North Miami ⑦

BISCAYNE PARK

MIAMI SHORES

Biscayne Bay

North Bay Village

MIAMI BEACH

① **Top 10 Sights**
see pp99–101

① **Places to Eat**
see p103

① **Independent Shops**
see p102

LITTLE HAITI

Area of Little Haiti map

0 km 2
0 miles 2

1 Little Haiti

MAP G2 ■ NE 2nd Ave, from about NE 55th to NE 80th ■ Marketplace: 5927 NE 2nd Ave ■ Haitian Heritage Museum: www.haitian heritagemuseum.org

Many Haitians have settled here since the 1980s. The Little Haiti Cultural Complex, housed in the Caribbean Marketplace, is the heart of the community. The building has brightly colored ironwork inspired by the Iron Market in Port-au-Prince, Haiti. Further south in the Design District is the Haitian Heritage Museum.

2 Bal Harbour

MAP H2

The Barrier islands north of Miami Beach are occupied mainly by luxury residential areas. Known for its flashy hotels and one of the swankiest malls, Bal Harbour is said to have more millionaires per capita than any other city in the US. On Collins Avenue, Bal Harbour Shops is particularly fancy. Elsewhere along 96th Street are galleries, gourmet shops, and many plastic surgery studios.

3 Ancient Spanish Monastery

MAP H1 ■ 16711 W Dixie Hwy, North Miami Beach ■ 305 945 1461 ■ Open 10am–4pm Wed & Thu (to 2pm Fri & Sat), 2–5pm Sun ■ Adm ■ www.spanishmonastery.com

This monastery is the oldest European-tradition building in the Western Hemisphere, originally built in 1133–41 near Segovia, Spain. In 1925, William Randolph Hearst

Ancient Spanish Monastery

bought the magnificent cloisters, had them dismantled stone by stone, and sent to the US, where the stones were reassembled in the early 1950s for $1.5 million. Call before visiting on weekends as the monastery will close for events such as weddings.

4 Sunny Isles Beach

MAP H1 ■ Hwy A1A (north of Haulover Park)

The resort of Sunny Isles Beach is lined with high-rise hotels and condos, built along the gorgeous beachfront. Landmark buildings include the residential Porsche Design Tower and its high-tech robotic parking garage. The area has a large expat Russian community, with caviar shops and Russian delis, restaurants, beauty salons, and real estate companies underscoring the area's nickname "Little Moscow."

Aerial view over Sunny Isles Beach

5 Design District

MAP G2 ■ Nr Buena Vista between NE 36th–41st sts and from NE 2nd to N Miami aves ■ www.miami designdistrict.net

It started out as a pineapple grove, but from the 1920s this zone was being called Decorators' Row because of the design stores that had moved in. For a while in the 1980s, due to high crime, the area fell on hard times, but things improved, and top-end design, furniture, and fixture shops once again rule. Most artists have moved here to escape the high rents of South Beach.

Design District luxury furniture store

6 Wynwood Arts District

MAP G3 ■ Bounded by N 36th St, N 20th St, I-95, and NW 1st Ave ■ www.wynwoodmiami.com

The former industrial warehouse district of Wynwood has been transformed into a vibrant neighborhood of art galleries, museums, clubs, and studios. Since 2009, huge murals – dubbed the Wynwood Walls (see p72) – have been a major element of the district's appeal.

DOWNTOWN MIAMI

Visitors to Greater Miami will notice both its serious wealth and extreme poverty, often displayed within a stone's throw of each other. Many under-privileged African American communities, as well as struggling immigrants from places like Cuba, Haiti, and other Central American countries, endure substandard living conditions in quarters of endless urban blight.

7 Museum of Contemporary Art North Miami

MAP G2 ■ 770 NE 125th St ■ 305 893 6211 ■ Open 10am–5pm Tue–Sun ■ Adm ■ www.mocanomi.org

The Museum of Contemporary Art opened its state-of-the-art building in 1996. It's known for its provocative exhibitions and for seeking a fresh approach in examining the art of our time. The permanent collection features emerging and established artists from the US and abroad.

8 Haulover Park and Beach

MAP H1 ■ 10800 Collins Ave ■ 305 947 3525

Haulover Park contains one of south Florida's most beautiful beaches – a mile and a half of golden sand drawing people from all walks of life. Nestled between the Intercoastal Waterway and the Atlantic, the beach is ideal for surfing and swimming, and on warm weekends it is jam-packed with sunbathers. The park itself has a marina, restaurant, tennis courts, a nine-hole golf course, and a kite shop. It is one of the nation's top ten nude beaches.

⑨ Arch Creek Park and Museum

MAP G2 ■ 1855 NE 135th St

Created around a natural limestone bridge formation, this location stands on ground that was once an important Native American trail. A museum/nature center contains artifacts left by Tequesta and Seminole peoples. Take a guided eco-tour to learn about endemic species.

Relaxing on the lawn, Greynolds Park

⑩ Greynolds Park

MAP H1 ■ 17530 W Dixie Hwy

An oak-shaded haven for runners, golfers, and other outdoor enthusiasts, Greynolds Park is landscaped with native and non-native plants, which include mangrove, royal palm, sea grape, palmetto, pampas grass, and gumbo limbo. You'll also find beach volleyball courts, a kids' playground, and plenty of picnic tables.

Wynwood Walls mural by artist, Case

A TOUR OF THE ANCIENT SPANISH MONASTERY

▶ MORNING

Drive north from central Miami on Highway 1 (also known as Biscayne Boulevard). The road is lined with shops – stop off at any that catch your eye. Turn left on NE 163rd Street, then right onto W Dixie Highway (also NE 22nd Avenue). The **Ancient Spanish Monastery** (see p99) is on the right after the canal. You may well feel a sense of awe as you walk around this beautiful little piece of medieval Europe on US soil. Even European visitors, who will have visited many such buildings in their homeland, marvel at the dedication of Hearst to put it here. For the best route through the grounds, start at the gift shop/museum, exit to the patio, then through the gardens, cloisters, and interior rooms, culminating at the chapel. Among the notable sights along the route are a 12th-century birdbath, a life-size statue of the Spanish king Alphonso VII (the monastery was constructed to commemorate one of his victories over the Moors), and two of only three known surviving round stained-glass windows, also from the 12th century.

AFTERNOON

In keeping with the Spanish theme, eat at nearby **Paquito's Mexican Restaurant** (see p103) and take a detour along NE 2nd Avenue through **Little Haiti** (see p99) on your way back.

See map on p98 ←

Independent Shops

Eclectic range of clothes at Intermix

natural and carved semi-precious gemstones, insects, shells, butterflies, skulls, animal mounts, and more.

1 Intermix
MAP H2 ■ Bal Harbour Shops, 9700 Collins Ave ■ 305 993 1232

Outfits for the discerning woman, whether 18 or 50. A great range of prices, labels, and accessories.

2 Addict
MAP H2 ■ Bal Harbour Shops, 9700 Collins Ave ■ 305 864 1099

Fashion sneakers for all the family, including rare sneakers not widely available in department stores.

3 Pinko
MAP H2 ■ Bal Harbour Shops, 9700 Collins Ave ■ 786 577 7330

Italian fashion brand, Pinko's unique and eclectic collection of women's apparel and accessories is fabulous.

4 Psycho Bunny
MAP H1 ■ Aventura Mall, 19501 Biscayne Blvd

This popular New York menswear brand with a captivating name has a huge cult following. The branch located in Aventura Mall sells its trademark polos, T-shirts, and hoodies.

5 Art By God
MAP G3 ■ 1280 NW 74th St

Impressive mineral/nature store, with dinosaur fossils,

6 Rebel
MAP G2 ■ 7648 Biscayne Blvd ■ 305 793 4104

Shoppers are bound to find something they want at Rebel, a high-end boutique that carries everything from everyday fashion to evening dresses.

7 Nini & Loli
MAP H1 ■ Aventura Mall, 19501 Biscayne Blvd

This local Miami store specializes in baby gear, strollers, car seats, furniture, diaper bags, toys, apparel, and all the baby basics.

8 Rasool's Menswear
MAP G2 ■ 6301 NW 7th Ave ■ 305 759 1250

Famous for its sleek Italian suits for men, the store also stocks urban wear, wedding tuxedos, and T-shirts with creative artwork on them.

9 Upper Buena Vista
MAP G2 ■ 184 NE 50th Terrace ■ 305 539 9555

An indoor-outdoor shopping mall with plant-filled home decor stores, local artisan shops, and plenty of cafés to keep you fueled.

10 Jalan Jalan
MAP G2 ■ 3600 NE 2nd Ave ■ 305 572 9998

The owners constantly change this home design showroom to add global artisan pieces made of petrified wood, Belgian glass, and Indian marble work.

Pots from Jalan Jalan

Places to Eat

PRICE CATEGORIES

For a three-course meal for one with half
a bottle of wine (or equivalent meal),
taxes, and extra charges.

$ under $35 $$ $35–$70 $$$ over $70

 Sugarcane Raw Bar Grill
MAP G2 ■ 3252 NE 1st Ave
■ 786 369 0353 ■ $$

Elegantly understated, Sugarcane
expertly prepares small plates of
meat and vegetables, cooked on
a Japanese robata grill. It also
offers an array of raw bar items
and delicious sushi.

2 Chez Le Bebe
MAP G2 ■ 114 NE 54th St
■ 305 751 7639 ■ $

A Little Haiti no-frills establishment
with traditional Haitian food, from
tender *griot* (fried pork) to stewed
goat; all plates come with rice,
beans, plantain, and salad.

**3 Michael's Genuine
Food and Drink**
MAP G2 ■ 130 NE 40th St ■ 305
676 0894 ■ $$

The best restaurant in Miami's
Design District has a unique menu,
serving a range of fresh seafood
dishes, woodfired pizzas and
tempting brunch cocktails.

4 Clive's Cafe
MAP G2 ■ 5890 NW 2nd Ave
■ 305 757 6512 ■ $

A popular and good-value Jamaican
restaurant in the heart of Little
Haiti, serving delicious classics such
as jerk chicken and curry goat, as
well as salt fish for breakfast.

5 Panther Coffee
MAP G3 ■ 2390 NW 2nd Ave
■ 305 677 3952 ■ $

Miami's wildly popular small-batch
coffee roaster operates this café
in the Wynwood Arts District, with
local art on the walls and a menu
of cakes, cookies, and savory snacks.

6 Lemoni Café
MAP G2 ■ 4600 NE 2nd Ave
■ 305 571 5080 ■ $

Cozy Design District café serving
wholesome food with a Mediterranean
slant, which is influenced by the
chef's French/Moroccan background.

7 Buena Vista Deli
MAP G2 ■ 4590 NE 2nd Ave
■ 305 576 3945 ■ $

Charming café in the Design District
serving homemade pastries and
coffee for breakfast, gourmet sandwiches on artisan-crafted breads for
lunch, and lighter fare for dinner.

Pretty patio, Mandolin Aegean Bistro

8 Mandolin Aegean Bistro
MAP G2 ■ 4312 NE 2nd Ave
■ 305 749 9140 ■ $$

This stylish Design District bistro
recreates simple, rustic dishes
from Greece and Turkey.

**9 Paquito's Mexican
Restaurant**
MAP G1 ■ 16265 Biscayne Blvd
■ 786 321 4952 ■ $$

Expect fresh tortilla soup, steak
Paquitos sautéed in a jalapeño and
onion sauce, and a yummy *mole verde*.

10 Andiamo!
MAP G2 ■ 5600 Biscayne Blvd
■ 305 762 5751 ■ $

Mouthwatering, brick-oven pizza
pies with a dizzying variety of top-
pings, as well as salads, paninis,
and a selection of local beers.

See map on p98

TOP 10 Coral Gables and Coconut Grove

Together Coral Gables and Coconut Grove constitute one of the most upscale neighborhoods in Greater Miami. The former was built by the real-estate developer George Merrick, who envisioned one of the first and most successfully planned suburbs in the US. Known as the "City Beautiful," it earns its moniker from winding avenues lined with elegant villas. Luxurious mansions and sailboats anchored in Biscayne Bay typify affluent Coconut Grove, where dining at a sidewalk cafe is a quintessential experience. The area has been constantly evolving since the countercultural days of the 1960s, and today its lively street scene makes it one of Miami's most vibrant districts.

Decorative lamp stand, Vizcaya Museum and Gardens

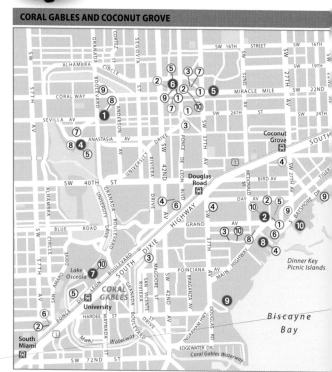

CORAL GABLES AND COCONUT GROVE

Merrick's beautiful Venetian Pool

1 Venetian Pool
MAP G3

This is one of the loveliest and most evocative of Merrick's additions to his vision for Coral Gables. The pool *(see p24)* is fed by springs and was the site of at least one movie starring Esther Williams, the 1940s water-ballet beauty.

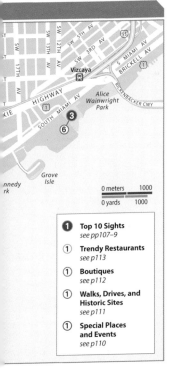

Grove Isle

Alice Wainwright Park

Vizcaya

1 Top 10 Sights
see pp107–9

1 Trendy Restaurants
see p113

1 Boutiques
see p112

1 Walks, Drives, and Historic Sites
see p111

1 Special Places and Events
see p110

2 CocoWalk
MAP G3 ■ 3015 Grand Ave
■ www.cocowalk.com

A five-story retail and entertainment venue in the heart of Coconut Grove that features 150,000 square feet of shops, restaurants, and more *(see p110)*. The atmosphere here is that of a village, with shops hanging out, zipping by on in-line skates and bikes, or clustering around the landscaped outdoor plaza where live music often happens. The main attractions in the evening are probably the hip bars and the large multiplex cinema.

3 Vizcaya Museum and Gardens

A historic and beautiful place *(see pp20–21)*; this icon of the city's cultural life is not to be missed.

4 The Biltmore
MAP F3

One of the grandest hotels in Florida, the Biltmore *(see p24)* opened in 1926. It's a fabulous Spanish Revival pile with a tower inspired by the Giralda in Sevilla. Herculean pillars line the grand lobby, and from the terrace you can survey the largest hotel swimming pool in the country. Johnny Weismuller, who played Tarzan, used to teach swimming here, and the likes of Al Capone, Judy Garland, and the Roosevelts came here in its heyday. Weekly tours of the hotel and grounds depart from the front desk.

The Biltmore, a Coral Gables hallmark

5 Miracle Mile
MAP F3–G3 ■ Coral Way
between Douglas & Le Jeune

In 1940, a developer hyped the town's main shopping street by naming it Miracle Mile. Colorful canopies adorn shops as prim and proper as their clientele. Stop to admire the Colonnade Building, at No. 133-169, with its splendid rotunda, fountain, and impressive Corinthian columns. Then move ahead to the nearby Salzedo Street, where you will find the Old Police and Fire Station (c.1939), with its square-jawed sculpted firemen.

6 Coral Gables Museum
MAP G3 ■ 285 Aragon Ave,
Coral Gables ■ 305 603 8067
■ Open 11am–5pm Tue–Fri & Sun,
10am–6pm Sat ■ www.coralgables
museum.org

Visit this fascinating museum to learn more about how Coral Gables developed over time, and about George Merrick's contribution to the area. Housed in the Old Police and Fire Station building, this civic arts complex features a beautiful and expansive public courtyard, along with the Fewell Gallery. The complex hosts exhibits devoted to the city's rich, historical, and architectural heritage. Permanent exhibits here present a remark-able display of the history of the Tamiami Trail that does not shy away from describing its devastating impact on the Everglades.

Asian collection, Lowe Art Museum

7 Lowe Art Museum
With around 19,500 pieces, Greater Miami's finest art museum features collections of both ancient and modern world art (see pp26–7).

8 Barnacle Historic State Park
MAP G3 ■ 3485 Main Hwy, Coconut Grove ■ 305 442 6866 ■ Open 9am–5pm Fri–Wed ■ 1-hour tours at 10 & 11:30am, 1 & 2:30pm ■ Adm ■ www.floridastateparks.org

Hidden away from the highway by a tropical hardwood hammock (mound) in Barnacle Historic State Park, this is Dade County's oldest home. It was designed and built in 1891 by Commodore Ralph Munroe, who made his living as a boat builder and a wrecker (salvager). In fact, wood from shipwrecks was used to build the house, and it was inventively laid out to allow the circulation of air, all-important in the days before air-conditioning. Rooms are packed with family heirlooms, old tools, and wonder-fully dated appliances, such as an early refrigerator.

The house at Barnacle Historic State Park

9 The Kampong

MAP G4 ▪ 4013 Douglas Rd
▪ 305 442 7169 ▪ Open only by appt,
check website ▪ www.ntbg.org

Just southwest of Coconut Grove,
the Kampong is one of Miami's lesser-
visited attractions. This botanical
garden was created by explorer and
horticulturist David Fairchild. He
bought the estate in 1916, spending
the next 40 years developing a collection of more than 5,000 tropical
flowers, fruit trees, and plants,
with an emphasis on Asia. The site
includes the Fairchild-Sweeney
House, built in 1928 in a combination
of Spanish and Southeast Asian styles.

Arched entrance into the Kampong

10 Dinner Key

MAP G3 ▪ 5 Bayshore Dr

The name derives from the early
days when settlers had picnics here.
In the 1930s, Pan American Airways
transformed Dinner Key into the
busiest seaplane base in the US.
It was also the departure point for
Amelia Earhart's doomed round-
the-world flight in 1937. You can still
see the airline's sleek Streamline
Moderne terminal, housing the
Miami City Hall; the hangars where
seaplanes were harbored are now
mostly boatyards. The marina here
is the most prestigious in Miami,
and berths many luxurious yachts.

A TOUR OF COCONUT GROVE VILLAGE

▶ MORNING

This walk is designed for
Wednesday to Monday, because it
begins with a tour of the **Barnacle
Historic State Park**. Try to get
there for the 10am tour, and
take note of the distinctive roof,
which gives the house its name.
As you exit, turn left and go
down to the corner of Devon Road
to enjoy the beautiful Mission-
style **Plymouth Congregational
Church**, built in 1916. If they're
open, pop into the back gardens.
Walk back along Main Highway
several blocks to No. 3500, the
Coconut Grove Playhouse, which
although not used, is a handsome
Mediterranean Revival building
that dominates the corner at
Charles Avenue. Continue along
Main Highway to the next street,
then stop for lunch and top-notch
people-watching at the ever-busy
GreenStreet Café *(see p110)*.

AFTERNOON

After lunch, walk up Commodore
Plaza to visit **Fashionista** *(see
p112)*. Afterwards, continue
on to Grand Avenue and turn
right; go down a few blocks
to the major intersection and
cross the street into the shopping mecca **CocoWalk** *(see p107)*.
On the next block, Rice Street,
look up to admire the fanciful
facade of the tree-lined streets
of **Mayfair in the Grove** mall
(2911 Grand Avenue). To finish
off your tour, visit nearby **Bombay
Darbar** *(see p113)* for dinner.
This Indian restaurant serves
some of the best curries and
kebabs in Miami.

See map on pp106–7 ➤

Special Places and Events

Stacked shelves at Books and Books

1 Books and Books
One of Greater Miami's best bookstores, this is set amid graceful arcades *(see p112)*.

2 Titanic Brewing Company
This popular Coral Gables brewpub *(see p113)* offers six styles of house brews on tap, along with 25 varieties of seasonal beers. It also hosts regular live music performances.

3 GreenStreet Café

MAP G3 ■ 3468 Main Hwy, Coconut Grove ■ 305 444 0244
Almost always crowded, this corner venue on Commodore Plaza is a prime people-watching spot in the Grove.

4 CocoWalk
A compact shopping and entertainment center *(see p107)* in Coconut Grove – always something or someone to catch the eye.

5 Watsco Center

MAP G3 ■ 1245 Dauer Dr, Coral Gables ■ www.watscocenter.com
This modern multi-purpose arena on the University of Miami campus seats 8,000 for a variety of recreational events, from college basketball to rock concerts.

6 Coconut Grove Arts Festival
MAP G3 ■ Third weekend in Feb ■ Throughout the Grove, especially Bayshore and Peacock Parks ■ www.cgaf.com
This festival attracts visitors who come to eat, drink, listen to concerts in Peacock Park, and browse among 300 arts and crafts booths.

7 Tamiami International Orchid Festival
Jan ■ www.tamiamiorchid festival.com
Florida has become one of the world centers for the orchid industry. More than half a million blooms are exhibited, with different themes every year.

8 Miami-Bahamas Goombay Festival
MAP G3 ■ Mid-May/early Jun ■ Throughout the Grove ■ www.coconutgrovebahamiangoombay festival.com
Known as the biggest African American heritage festival in the US, this party includes a parade, Caribbean music, Island food, and *junkanoo* dancers.

9 Columbus Day Regatta
MAP G3 ■ Mid-Oct ■ Coral Reef Yacht Club to Elliot Key ■ www.columbusdayregatta.net
Some 600 boats take part in this fun sailing celebration.

10 King Mango Strut
MAP G3 ■ Early Jan ■ Starts at Main Hwy & Commodore Plaza, Coconut Grove ■ www.kingmango strut.org
Outrageous tradition that sends up the year's events and celebrities, harking back to the days when the Grove was a haven for intellectuals and eccentrics. The party climaxes with a concert and dance in Peacock Park.

See map on pp106–7

Walks, Drives, and Historic Sites

 Miracle Mile
Though not really quite a mile, nor particularly miraculous, this street (see p108) and the parallel ones are mostly about shops and restaurants, with some architectural interest.

 **Coconut Grove Village**
MAP G3
This is a lovely place to walk (see p109), with its vibrant community centered around CocoWalk.

 Merrick Villages
Driving around Coral Gables to take in these charming luxury residences (see pp24–5), done up in the styles of various national and regional cultures, will take perhaps a couple of hours to admire and fully appreciate.

 Barnacle Historic State Park
This unusual house (see p108) is the area's oldest, built in 1891.

 The Biltmore
Inimitably ornate and grand, this is one of the world's gorgeous hotels (see p107), another Merrick gem opened in 1926.

 Vizcaya Museum and Gardens
A recreation of a 16th-century Italian villa complemented by verdant, formal gardens (see pp20–21).

 Congregational Church
Merrick's deliciously Baroque paean to his father, a Congregational minister, was Coral Gables' first church (see p25) and remains the city's most beautiful to this day.

 Venetian Pool
Considered one of the world's most attractive public swimming pools (see p24). You could spend half a day enjoying its charms. Children under the age of three are not allowed.

9 Coral Gables Merrick House
MAP G3 ▪ 907 Coral Way ▪ 305 460 5093 ▪ Open for guided tours only: 1pm, 2pm, & 3pm Sat & Sun ▪ Adm
The restored boyhood home of George Merrick (see p25) is remarkably modest compared to the grandeur of the dreams he realized. The city of Coral Gables took its name from this house. The stone to build it was quarried from what is now the Venetian Pool. The historic site is now a museum that houses exhibitions about Coral Gables and its surrounding area.

10 Lowe Art Museum
Originally founded in 1950, the Lowe Art Museum (see pp26–7) showcases ancient Egyptian, Greco-Roman, Asian, and American art through the 17th century to contemporary European and American art.

Looking back across the water to the east facade of Villa Vizcaya

Boutiques

 The Maya Hatcha
MAP G3 ▪ 2982 Grand Ave,
Coconut Grove
This funky little shop offers incense,
ethically made clothing, handmade
jewelry, and all things spiritual.

2 **Morays Jewelers**
MAP G3 ▪ 116 Miracle Mile,
Coral Gables
One of Miami's top jewelry shops,
Morays stocks a wide range of
watches, diamonds, pearls, and
colored gemstone pieces.

3 **Zoey Reva**
MAP G3 ▪ 133 Giralda Ave
▪ www.zoeyreva.com
A hidden gem in Coral Gables. Great
selection of stylish women's clothing,
with a fabulous line in patterned
dresses and loungewear.

 Islandgirl Miami
MAP G3 ▪ 330 San Lorenzo
Ave (Shops at Merrick Park)
Everything here has a tropical,
beachy theme, from the floral
dresses to the bikinis. It is all
created by local designers.

5 **Books and Books**
MAP G3 ▪ 265 Aragon Ave,
Coral Gables
One of a chain of stores across the
state, this bookshop specializes in arts
and literature, and books on Florida.
Here there's a great café, frequent
poetry readings, and book signings.

6 **White House
Black Market**
MAP G3 ▪ 350 San Lorenzo Ave,
Suite 2130
A rarified range of women's fashion.
Elegant cocktail dresses, tailored
suits, shoes, and accessories.

7 **Golden Triangle**
MAP G3 ▪ 2308 Galiano St,
Coral Gables
New Age boutique stocking imported
Asian items: incense, jewelry, Tibetan
bowls, Buddha statues, beautiful
clothing, crystals, and more.

8 **Fashionista**
MAP G3 ▪ 3135 Commodore
Plaza, Coconut Grove
This is the place to pick up designer
merchandise, albeit slightly worn,
for a fraction of the price.

9 **Pepi Bertini**
MAP G3 ▪ 357 Miracle Mile,
Coral Gables ▪ 305 461 3374
Started in 1985 by Cuban-born Pepi
"Bertini" Gonzalez, this bespoke
Italian-style tailor shop specializes in
men's suits, shirts, and casual wear.

10 **Essence Boutique**
MAP G3 ▪ 78 Miracle Mile,
Coral Gables ▪ 305 448 6777
Upscale women's attire, with trendy
purses, shoes, and swimwear, and
quirky jewelry too.

A book reading at Books and Books

Trendy Restaurants

PRICE CATEGORIES

For a three-course meal for one with half a bottle of wine (or equivalent meal), taxes, and extra charges.

$ under $35 $$ $35–$70 $$$ over $70

① Pascal's on Ponce
MAP G3 ▪ 2611 Ponce de Leon Blvd, Coral Gables ▪ 305 444 2024 ▪ $$$

A perfect place for a romantic meal, with exquisite French cuisine by chef Pascal Oudin, fine linens, beautiful table settings, and attentive staff.

② Caffe Abbracci
MAP G3 ▪ 318 Aragon Ave, Coral Gables ▪ 305 441 0700 ▪ $$

Founded by Nino Pernetti, this restaurant offers a Mediterranean ambience and Italian comfort food. The menu has a variety of desserts as well as an extensive wine list.

③ Christy's
MAP G3 ▪ 3101 Ponce de Leon Blvd, Coral Gables ▪ 305 446 1400 ▪ $$$

A local favorite since its opening in 1978, this restaurant has been made a landmark by politicians, CEOs, and celebrities.

④ Berries in the Grove
MAP G3 ▪ 2884 SW 27th Ave, Coconut Grove ▪ 305 448 2111 ▪ $$

Locals have embraced this restaurant, which captures the best of Florida's sunshine and healthy cuisine – from a pizza to a tropical fruit smoothie.

⑤ Bombay Darbar
MAP G3 ▪ 2901 Florida Ave, Coconut Grove ▪ 305 444 7272 ▪ $$

Regarded as Miami's best Indian restaurant. The menu has kebabs, curries, and vegetarian options.

⑥ Titanic Brewing Company
MAP G3 ▪ 5813 Ponce de Leon Blvd, Coral Gables ▪ 305 667 2537 ▪ $

Lift a pint of homemade brew and sample crawfish or calamari snacks.

⑦ Kaia Greek Earth Grill
MAP G3 ▪ 232 Miracle Mile, Coral Gables ▪ 786 362 6997

Set in a breezy interior, filled with wicker and wood, Kaia Greek Earth Grill serves flavorful, upscale Mediterranean cuisine. Try the grilled octopus, calamari, hummus, and the unique cocktails.

⑧ Fontana
MAP F3 ▪ 1200 Anastasia Ave, Coral Gables ▪ 305 913 3201 ▪ $$$

This restaurant offers an excellent fine dining experience. Enjoy the exquisite Italian cuisine prepared by Italian chef Giuseppe "Beppe" Galazzi.

Sophisticated setting, Fontana

⑨ Isabelle's Grill Room & Garden
MAP G3 ▪ 3300 SW 27th Ave, Coconut Grove ▪ 305 644 4675 ▪ $$$

Located in the Ritz Carlton, this gourmet restaurant specializes in seafood. Try the sandwiches, mushroom pappardelle, or Florida snapper.

⑩ Le Bouchon du Grove
MAP G3 ▪ 3430 Main Hwy, Coconut Grove ▪ 305 448 6060 ▪ $$

Transporting diners to France for 20 years, this cozy bistro is renowned for its traditional Lyonnaise cuisine. It serves breakfast, lunch, and dinner.

See map on pp106–7

TOP 10 South of Coconut Grove

Heading south from Miami's main events, once you get past the nondescript suburbs, you enter tracts of citrus groves and tropical nurseries. The general atmosphere changes too – a bit more traditional and Old South. There is a great range of shopping opportunities, museums, parks and gardens. And you will discover educational attractions for kids and adults alike, including the Biscayne National Park.

Fairchild Tropical Botanic Garden

SOUTH OF COCONUT GROVE

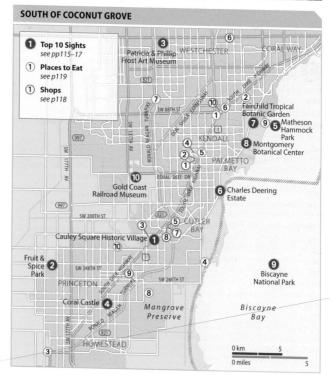

1 Top 10 Sights
see pp115–17

1 Places to Eat
see p119

1 Shops
see p118

3 Patricia & Phillip Frost Art Museum

6 WESTCHESTER   CORAL WAY

2 Fairchild Tropical Botanic Garden

KENDALL

8 Montgomery Botanical Center

Matheson Hammock Park

PALMETTO BAY

10 Gold Coast Railroad Museum

6 Charles Deering Estate

CUTLER BAY

Cauley Square Historic Village

2 Fruit & Spice Park

PRINCETON

4 Coral Castle

Mangrove Preserve

9 Biscayne National Park

Biscayne Bay

HOMESTEAD

0 km   5

0 miles   5

1 Cauley Square Historic Village

MAP E6 ▪ 22400 Old Dixie Hwy,
▪ 305 258 3543 ▪ Open 11am–5pm
Tue–Fri, 10am–6pm Sat & Sun
▪ www.cauleysquare.com

This 1903 railroad workers' settlement has been charmingly preserved, with restaurants, art galleries, and stores.

2 Fruit & Spice Park

MAP E5 ▪ 24801 Redland Rd
(SW 187th Ave), Homestead ▪ 305
247 5727 ▪ Open 9am–5pm daily
▪ Adm ▪ Guided tours

This 37-acre (15-ha) botanical park is devoted to tropical plants, such as citrus fruits, grapes, bananas, herbs, spices, nuts, and bamboo. The astonishing number of varieties on display include a selection of poisonous species and hundreds of bamboo and banana varieties. A wonderful store enables you to stock up your cupboards with many unusual fruit products.

3 Patricia & Phillip Frost Art Museum

MAP F3 ▪ 10975 SW 17th St ▪ 305 348
2890 ▪ Open 11am–5pm Tue–Sun
▪ 1-hour tours by reservation
▪ https://frost.fiu.edu

The museum specializes in Latin American and 20th-century American art and presents six to eight major exhibitions each year. The Avenue of the Arts displays sculptures by well-known artists in a landscaped open space at the center of the FIU (Florida International University) campus – a wonderfully rich and important representation of modern work. It is recognized nationally as one of the world's great collections of sculpture and the largest on a university campus. It includes major pieces by Alexander Liberman, Manuel Mendive, Pablo Atchugarry, and John Henry.

Bananas, Fruit & Spice Park

Coral Castle, carved from coral rock

4 Coral Castle

MAP E6 ▪ 28655 South
Dixie Hwy ▪ 305 248 6345 ▪ Open
9am–6pm Sun–Thu ▪ Adm ▪ www.
coralcastle.com

A castle it isn't, but a conundrum it is. From 1920 to 1940, Latvian immigrant Edward Leedskalnin built this mysterious pile as a valentine to a girl who had jilted him in 1913. No one knows how he single-handedly quarried and transported the 1,100 tons of tough coral rock, carved all the enormous chunks into monumental shapes, and set them all into place so flawlessly. One 9-ton gate is so exquisitely balanced that it opens with the pressure of your little finger.

5 Matheson Hammock Park

MAP G4 ▪ 9610 Old Cutler Rd
▪ 305 665 5475 ▪ Open sunrise–
sunset ▪ Adm

Perfect for families, this beach is surrounded by lush parkland laced with trails and a unique man-made atoll pool. When you're hungry, make for NOMA Beach at Redfish (see p119), set in a historic coral rock building dating from the 1930s.

Stone House, Charles Deering Estate

also serves as a botanical research institute. Around a series of man-made lakes stands one of the world's largest collections of palm trees, as well as countless other wonderful trees and plants. During a walking tour, guides describe how plants are used to manufacture everything from Chanel No. 5 to golf balls.

6 Charles Deering Estate

MAP F4 ▪ 16701 SW 72nd Ave, at SW 167th St & Old Cutler Rd ▪ 305 235 1668 ▪ Open 10am–4pm daily ▪ Adm ▪ www.deeringestate.org

Right on Biscayne Bay, the estate contains two significant architectural works: Richmond Cottage, built in 1896 as the area's first inn, and a large Mediterranean Revival "Stone House," which was built in 1922.

7 Fairchild Tropical Botanic Garden

MAP G4 ▪ 10901 Old Cutler Rd ▪ 305 667 1651 ▪ Open 10am–5pm daily ▪ Adm ▪ www.fairchildgarden.org

This dizzyingly beautiful tropical paradise was established in 1938 and

8 Montgomery Botanical Center

MAP G4 ▪ 11901 Old Cutler Rd, Coral Gables ▪ 305 667 3800, call ahead to book a visit ▪ www.montgomerybotanical.org

Formerly a private estate, this 120-acre park was created by Robert and Nell Montgomery, founders of the Fairchild Botanic Garden. Its aim is to advance science, education, conservation and knowledge of tropical plants for garden design. The vast collection of tropical plants focuses on palms and cycads from around the world.

9 Biscayne National Park

MAP G5 ▪ 9700 SW 328th St Homestead ▪ 305 230 1144 ▪ Visitor center: open 9am–5pm daily ▪ www.nps.gov/bisc

Biscayne National Park is 95 per cent water, therefore most visitors enter it by private boat. Otherwise, the Dante Fascell Visitor Center at Convoy Point is the only place in the

The Fairchild Tropical Botanic Garden

national park you can drive to and, from there, you have several boating options. The concession offers canoe rentals, glass-bottom boat tours, snorkel trips, scuba trips, and transportation to the island for campers. There's also a picturesque boardwalk that takes you along the shoreline out to the rock jetty beside the boat channel heading to the bay.

Engine, Gold Coast Railroad Museum

(10) Gold Coast Railroad Museum

MAP E4 ▪ 12450 SW 152nd St ▪ 305 253 0063 ▪ Open 10am–4pm Mon, Wed & Fri, 11am–4pm Sat & Sun ▪ Adm ▪ www.goldcoastrailroadmuseum.org

The museum was started in 1957 by a group of Miamians who were trying to save threatened pieces of Florida history. Some of the oldest items in the collection are the "Ferdinand Magellan," a private railroad car built for President Franklin Roosevelt; the FEC engine that pulled a rescue train out from Marathon after the 1935 hurricane; and the 113 locomotive built in 1913. The Edwin Link is a small-gauge children's railroad.

HURRICANE COUNTRY

One in ten North Atlantic hurricanes hits Florida – an average of one big storm every two years. In 2018, Hurricane Michael measured Category 5, the worst on the Saffir-Simpson Scale. In 2022, the Category 4 Hurricane Ian became the deadliest storm since 1935, making disastrous landfall in the populated areas of Fort Myers on the Gulf Coast.

DEERING ESTATE WALK

▶ MORNING

To get to the **Charles Deering Estate**, drive south from Miami on Highway 1 (Dixie Highway) and turn left on SW 168th Street. Follow it until it dead-ends at the estate on SW 72nd Avenue. A full tour of the grounds will take three to four hours. Follow the Entrance Trail to begin, and as you emerge from the mangroves you will encounter a splendid vista of Biscayne Bay. Note the water level marker showing the inundation caused by Hurricane Andrew in 1992. Richmond Cottage, the original structure here, was built as an inn in 1896. It was destroyed by Andrew, but has since been replicated. The elegant Stone House next door contains bronze and copper doors, portraits of the Deering family, a celebrated wine cellar, and more besides. Head over to the Carriage House, where you can see a vintage gas pump. If you have time, take the Main Nature Trail, which crosses a handsome coral rock bridge, built in 1918. Finally, walk out through the estate's historic Main Entrance, with its coral rock pillars, and wood and iron gates.

AFTERNOON

Picnicking on the grounds is a possibility, and some facilities are provided. Or, for a hearty lunch, take a short drive north to **Guadalajara** (see p119). To make a full day's visit, head south along Highway 1 to the eccentric **Coral Castle** (see p115).

See map on p114 ←

Shops

① Twice Vintage
MAP F4 ▪ The Falls Shopping Center #525A, US Hwy 1, 8888 SW 136th St ▪ 305 665 7620

Chic shop with home decor and vintage furniture pieces, as well as clothing and accessories.

The open-air Falls Shopping Center

② The Falls Shopping Center
MAP F4 ▪ US Hwy 1, SW 136th St ▪ 305 255 4571 ▪ www.simon.com/mall/the-falls

This is one of the largest open-air shopping, dining, and entertainment complexes in the country. There are over 100 stores set in a picturesque waterscape with tropical foliage.

③ Esmeralda's Earth Wind & Fire Boutique
MAP F5 ▪ 12345 SW 224th St ▪ www.earthwindandfire shop.com

This cottage store is packed with pretty little things such as incense, candles, crystals, and dream catchers.

④ Art Thyme
MAP F4 ▪ 8841 SW 132 St ▪ 305 992 8222 ▪ www.artthyme.com

Paint your own pottery or canvas at this friendly studio, which also offers clay modeling, mosaic making, and glass painting. It also sells take-home kits.

⑤ Survival Miami
MAP F5 ▪ 20505 South Dixie Hwy, Southland Mall ▪ 786 701 2140 ▪ www.survivalmiami.com

Urban and streetwear brand hailing from south Miami, with a focus on men's sneakers, graphic tees, hoodies, jackets, hats, and bags.

⑥ Miami Twice
MAP F3 ▪ 6562 SW 40th St ▪ 305 666 0127

Along with vintage clothing and jewelry, antique-hunters should visit Miami Twice to discover Art Deco items and other treasure.

⑦ Southland Mall
MAP F5 ▪ 20505 South Dixie Hwy ▪ www.mysouthlandmall.com

One of the biggest malls south of Miami houses the likes of Macy's, JC Penney, Old Navy, TJ Maxx, and Victoria's Secret, along with smaller local boutiques.

⑧ Claire's Boutique
MAP F5 ▪ 20505 South Dixie Hwy, Southland Mall ▪ 305 251 2307

Great gift items from women's earrings and bracelets to hair accessories and purses are sold at this great boutique.

⑨ Metropolis Comics
MAP E6 ▪ 27455 S Dixie Hwy, Store #4, Homestead ▪ 850 300 3816

Tucked inside the Niranja Lakes Shopping Center, this little gem offers a wide range of comic books, manga, anime, and video games. It has fresh shipments daily – DC comics arrive on Tuesdays, while Marvel are released on Wednesdays.

⑩ Voyage
MAP G3 ▪ 7535 N Kendall Dr, Dadeland Mall ▪ 786 773 3527 ▪ www.voyagemiami.co

This mini-chain specializes in high-quality luggage including travel wallets and suitcases.

Places to Eat

PRICE CATEGORIES

For a three-course meal for one with half a bottle of wine (or equivalent meal), taxes, and extra charges.

$ under $35 $$ $35–$70 $$$ over $70

Shorty's BBQ
MAP F4 ■ 9200 South Dixie Hwy ■ 305 670 7732 ■ $$

This South Florida minichain, set up in 1951 by E. L. "Shorty" Allen, is known for its barbecue chicken, pulled pork, and sumptuous baby-back ribs.

Whip N Dip Ice Cream
MAP G4 ■ 1407 Sunset Dr ■ 305 665 2565 ■ $

Hard-to-resist cakes and ice cream, made with locally sourced ingredients and created on site; think brownie batter, pumpkin pie, and toasted coconut

Robert Is Here
MAP E6 ■ 19200 SW 344th St, Homestead ■ 305 246 1592 ■ $

This legendary fruit stand (now a huge roadside store) has specialized in locally grown rare fruits since 1959. Also serves milkshakes and smoothies.

Black Point Ocean Grill
MAP F5 ■ 24775 SW 87th Ave, Cutler Bay ■ 305 258 3918 ■ $$

Lively restaurant overlooking Black Point Marina and Black Creek, with a menu of fresh seafood, fish tacos, salads, and sandwiches. Alfresco seating available.

5 Guadalajara
MAP F4 ■ 8461 SW 132nd St, Pinecrest ■ 786 242 4444 ■ $

Home-cooked Mexican fare in a characterful locale. Try dipping a tortilla in a *queso fundido* (cheese fondue). The portions are huge.

Two Chefs
MAP F4 ■ 8287 South Dixie Hwy ■ 305 663 2100 ■ $$

American and contemporary cuisine with international influences are served in a bistro-style setting.

7 The Melting Pot
MAP F4 ■ 11520 SW Sunset Dr ■ 305 279 8816 ■ $$

A relaxed atmosphere with private tables. The menu ranges from vegetarian dishes to filet mignon.

8 Sweet Delights
MAP E6 ■ 23135 South Dixie Hwy ■ 786 339 9790 ■ $

The best place in South Miami to buy Key lime pie, with at least 16 different varieties to try – customers are encouraged to taste samples first.

Breezy outdoor seating at NOMA Beach

9 NOMA Beach at Redfish
MAP G4 ■ 9610 Old Cutler Rd ■ 305 668 8788 ■ $$

One of Miami's most romantic spots (see p45), nestled amid the tropical magic of Matheson Hammock Park. Fresh seafood and coastal Italian dishes are prepared by celebrity chef Donatella Arpaia.

10 Redland Ranch
MAP E5 ■ 14655 SW 232nd St, South Miami ■ 786 493 2805 ■ $

Tropical produce store with a cult following, offering juices, shakes, smoothies, sandwiches, and fruits.

See map on p114 ←

ⓘ⓿ The Keys

Helmet, Mel Fisher Maritime Museum

The Florida Keys are a string of wild, variegated gems hung in a necklace of liquid turquoise. This is a place for outdoor activities: watersports of all kinds, sportfishing, and hiking through the nature preserves and virgin tropical forests. These islands also have abundant wildlife, including unique flora and fauna, as evidenced by the many parks and family attractions focusing on encounters with nature. Even so, at least 20 different species of Keys plant and animal life are endangered or threatened.

Along the only route (US 1) that takes you from the mainland all the way out to Key West, you'll find everything from plush resorts to roadside stands selling wonderful home-grown produce.

THE KEYS

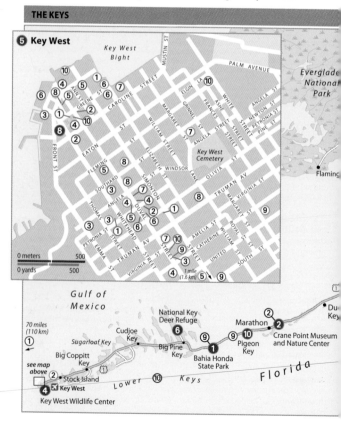

1 Bahia Honda State Park

MAP B6 ■ 36850 Overseas Hwy, Big Pine Key ■ 305 872 2353 ■ Open 8am–sunset daily ■ Adm ■ www.floridastateparks.org/bahiahonda

This protected area has the finest beaches in the Keys – and is voted among the best in the US. Brilliantly white sand is backed by tropical forest crossed by nature trails.

2 Crane Point Museum and Nature Center

MAP C6 ■ 5550 Overseas Hwy, Marathon ■ 305 743 9100 ■ Open 9am–5pm Mon–Sat, noon–5pm Sun ■ Adm ■ www.cranepoint.net

You can see a 600-year-old dugout canoe, remnants of pirate ships, a simulated coral reef cave, and the Bellarmine jug (c 1580), a shipwreck artifact in almost perfect condition here. There's also a gift shop and the colorful Marathon Wild Bird Center.

John Pennekamp Coral Reef State Park

3 John Pennekamp Coral Reef State Park

MAP D5 ■ MM 102.5 Key Largo ■ 305 451 6300 ■ Open 8am–sunset daily ■ Adm ■ www.pennekamppark.com

The park is known for its fabulous coral reef life. You can rent canoes, dinghies, or motorboats, as well as snorkeling and scuba gear, or choose a glass-bottom boat ride. Most destinations are actually in the neighboring Florida Keys (Key Largo) National Marine Sanctuary. The shallow waters of Dry Rocks are especially good for snorkeling, as is the nearby Molasses Reef.

4 Key West Wildlife Center

MAP A6 ■ 1801 White St ■ Open 11am–2pm Thu–Tue ■ www.keywestwildlifecenter.org

This wildlife rehabilitation center and nature reserve, located in the 7-acre-(3-ha-) Indigenous Park in Key West, provides refuge for marine and land mammals, wild birds, sea turtles, and tortoises. Wander the pleasant, meandering nature trail.

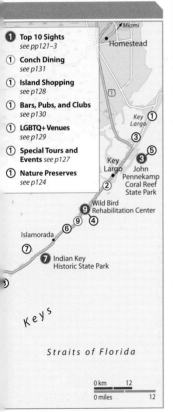

1 Top 10 Sights see pp121–3
1 Conch Dining see p131
1 Island Shopping see p128
1 Bars, Pubs, and Clubs see p130
1 LGBTQ+ Venues see p129
1 Special Tours and Events see p127
1 Nature Preserves see p124

Miami
Homestead
Key Largo
Key Largo
John Pennekamp Coral Reef State Park
Wild Bird Rehabilitation Center
Islamorada
Indian Key Historic State Park
Keys
Straits of Florida

0 km 12
0 miles 12

Custom House Museum, Key West

⑤ Key West

Rich in breathtaking beauty and in history, the self-styled Conch (pronounced "konk") Republic seems truly a world apart from the rest of the United States *(see pp32–3)*.

⑥ National Key Deer Refuge

MAP B6 ■ 30587 Overseas Hwy, Big Pine Key ■ 305 872 0774 ■ Open 24 hrs daily

Spanning a varied landscape of pine forest, mangroves, tropical hardwood hammocks, and fresh- and salt-water wetlands, this refuge is home to 23 endangered and threatened species of flora and fauna, including the Key deer. As a consequence of poaching and loss of habitats, fewer than 50 of these diminutive creatures were left until this refuge was established in 1957. Now there are estimated to be about 600. Drive very slowly and don't feed them.

⑦ Indian Key Historic State Park

MAP C5 ■ Offshore Island, Islamorada ■ 305 664 2540 ■ Open 8am–sunset daily ■ www.floridastateparks.org/indiankey

Tiny Indian Key has a surprisingly large amount of history for its size (10.5 acres/4.25 ha). An ancient Native American site, it was settled in 1831 by Captain J. Houseman, an opportunistic wrecker. In 1840 Seminoles attacked, killing the settlers. The Key was abandoned, and today only the outlines of the village remain, overgrown by vegetation. These are the descendants of plants belonging to Dr. Henry Perrine, a botanist who was killed in the raid.

⑧ Mel Fisher Maritime Museum

MAP A6 ■ 200 Greene St, Key West ■ 305 294 2633 ■ Open 10am–4pm daily ■ Adm ■ www.melfisher.org

The maritime museum displays treasure salvaged from shipwrecks from the late 15th to the mid-18th centuries, when Europeans explored what was to them the "New World." Their exploits, their commerce, and their impact on the Indigenous peoples of the Americas can be understood in the artifacts in this museum's collection. Its four ships include the *Nuestra Señora de Atocha*, which sank off Florida in 1622, and the *Henrietta Marie*, an English galleon that sank off the Florida Keys in 1700.

THE KEYS: MYTH AND MAGIC

The very name conjures up visions of windswept seascapes and wild goings-on: Humphrey Bogart and Lauren Bacall in the classic melodrama, *Key Largo*; some of the greatest US writers (Ernest Hemingway, Tennessee Williams, et al.) finding their muses where the US meets the Caribbean; and a free, unfettered lifestyle too good to be true.

⑨ Florida Keys Wild Bird Rehabilitation Center

MAP C5 ■ 92080 Overseas Hwy, Tavernier ■ Open sunrise–sunset daily ■ www.missionwildbird.com

This refuge for native and migratory birds comprises a bird hospital and education center, and a bird sanctuary – 12 acres (5 ha) of wetlands providing a natural habitat for over 120 resident rescued birds, and other flourishing native flora and fauna.

Egret, Florida Keys Wild Bird Rehabilitation Center

⑩ Pigeon Key

MAP B6 ■ 2010 Overseas Hwy, Marathon ■ 305 743 5999 ■ Open 9:30am–4pm daily ■ Adm ■ www.pigeonkey.net

This was the site of the work camp for those who built Henry M. Flagler's Overseas Railroad Bridge, described as the eighth wonder of the world when completed in 1912. A marine research foundation has been established in the old buildings. Take the ferry to get to the island.

Bird's-eye view of Pigeon Key

A DAY'S WALK ON KEY WEST

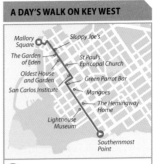

▶ MORNING

Begin at about 10am. Start at the Southernmost Point in continental US, overlooking the Atlantic at the intersection of Whitehead and South streets, where the marker informs you that Cuba is only 90 miles (144 km) away. Then head up Whitehead to the **Lighthouse Museum** *(see p33)* and climb its 88 steps for a great overview of the island and beyond. Next stop is the **Hemingway Home** *(see p32)*, at No. 907; here you can take in a nostalgic trip through the writer's life as a Conch. Then move on to the **Green Parrot Bar** *(see p130)*, at No. 601 Whitehead, to admire its age-old funkiness and have a drink before lunch. From here, head over to Duval Street, to **Mangoes** restaurant *(see p131)*, at No. 700, for a great lunch and stellar people-watching.

AFTERNOON

Admire the Spanish Colonial facade of the San Carlos Institute, and, on the next block up, the lovely stained-glass windows of St. Paul's Episcopal Church. At No. 322, visit the Oldest House Museum and Garden. Now things might get very "Key West," as you climb to the third floor of the **Bull and Whistle Bar** *(see p130)* to find the **Garden of Eden** *(see p57)*, a clothing-optional bar (no cameras or cell phones). Farther along stop at historic **Sloppy Joe's** *(see p130)*. By now, it should be time for the famous sunset celebration, so head down to Mallory Square *(see p32)*.

See map on pp120–21 ←

Nature Preserves

1 Key Largo Hammock Botanical State Park

MAP D5 ▪ Country Rd 905, MM 106 ▪ 305 676 3777 ▪ Open sunrise–sunset daily ▪ Adm

The largest remaining tropical West Indian hardwood and mangrove hammock is a refuge for protected indigenous flora and fauna.

2 Crane Point Museum and Nature Center

Walk the nature trails to Florida Bay and check out the Crane Point Museum and Nature Center and the Adderly Town Historic Site *(see p121)*.

3 Crocodile Lake Wildlife Refuge

MAP D5 ▪ 10750 County Rd 905, Key Largo ▪ 305 451 4223 ▪ Open sunrise–sunset daily

Part of the United States National Wildlife Refuge System, this sanctuary for the endangered American crocodiles is itself closed to the public, but on site there is an information kiosk and a pleasant native pollinator garden for visitors to enjoy.

4 Florida Keys Wild Bird Rehabilitation Center

A safe haven *(see p123)* for recovering Keys sea birds, including hawks, pelicans, herons, and owls.

5 John Pennekamp Coral Reef State Park

Most famous for its stunning offshore coral reef *(see p121)*, where snorkeling, scuba diving, and glass-bottom boat rides are great favorites.

6 Windley Key Fossil Reef State Geological Park

MAP C5 ▪ 84900 Overseas Hwy, Islamorada ▪ 305 664 2540 ▪ Open 8am–5pm Thu–Mon ▪ Adm

There are nature displays in the center of the park and trails lead into the railroad's old quarries, where you can discover exquisite pieces of fossilized brain coral and sea ferns.

7 Lignumvitae Key Botanical State Park

MAP C5 ▪ 77200 Overseas Hwy, Islamorada ▪ 305 664 2540 ▪ Park: open 8am–4pm Thu–Mon; ferry: 1–4pm Fri–Sun

Access is only by boat to this beautiful virgin hardwood forest home and gardens built by William Matheson.

8 Long Key State Park

MAP C6 ▪ 67400 Overseas Hwy, Long Key ▪ 305 664 4815 ▪ Open 8am–sunset daily ▪ Adm

The boardwalk at Long Key cuts through a mangrove swamp, where you can see waterbirds.

9 Bahia Honda State Park

Heavily forested and with great nature trails, this park *(see p121)* offers sublime snorkeling experiences.

10 Looe Key National Marine Sanctuary

MAP B6 ▪ MM 27.5 oceanside ▪ 305 872 3210

One of the Keys' most spectacular coral reefs, Looe Key is great for snorkeling and diving. Call for boat trips to the best spots.

Kids playing, John Pennekamp Park

Plants and Animals in the Keys

 Coral
Although it appears to be an insensate rock, coral is actually a living organism of various species, and a very fragile one at that, easily damaged by the slightest touch.

 Palms
Although only a few species of palms are natives in the Keys – the royal palm, the sabal palm, the saw palmetto, and the thatch palm – a huge range of imported palms now adorn the islands.

 Egrets
Often visible on the islands, and similar to herons, are the great egret, the snowy egret (distinguishable by its black legs and yellow feet), and the reddish egret.

 Double-Crested Cormorant
Notable for its S-curved neck, distinctive beak, and spectacular diving skills, this is one of the most fascinating of Keys birds.

 White Ibis
Recognizable for its long, down-curving beak, this medium-sized white wading bird, numerous in Florida, was sacred to the Egyptians.

 Key Deer
The diminutive Key deer are found primarily on Big Pine and No Name keys. These tiny, docile creatures reach a maximum height of about 30 in (80 cm).

 Herons
These elegant long-legged birds include the great blue heron, the white phase heron, the little blue heron, the tricolored heron, the green-backed heron, and the black-crowned night heron.

Gumbo limbo, noted for its red bark

8 Gumbo Limbo Tree
Called the "tourist tree" due to its red and peeling bark which resembles sunburnt skin, this unmistakable species – a Florida native – is found all over the Keys.

9 Threatened and Endangered Species
The Florida Keys conceal many endangered species. These include the American crocodile, Schaus swallowtail butterfly, Key Largo wood rat and cotton mouse, and roseate spoonbill, all of which have either been hunted near to the point of extinction or lost their habitats due to human encroachment.

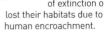

Roseate spoonbill in flight

10 Sea Turtles
These long-lived creatures come in a wide variety of shapes and sizes. From the largest to the smallest they are the leatherback, the loggerhead, the green, the hawksbill, and the Ridley turtles.

See map on pp120–21

Sports Activities in the Keys

1 **Swimming**
Some of the best beaches in the world are in the Keys. Don't worry if the ocean temperature falls below the usual 79° F (26° C) – most hotels have heated swimming pools.

2 **Fishing**
Good Times Key West: 305 923 3635; www.goodtimeskeywest.com
The Keys are a paradise for deep-sea fishing. With the Gulf Stream nearby, these waters offer the most varied fishing imaginable. Boat trips are easy to come by; try Good Times Key West.

3 **Water-Skiing and Jet-Skiing**
Sunset Watersports: 305 296 2554; www.sunsetwatersportskeywest.com
Water-skiing and jet-skiing are available wherever there's a marina, especially in developed tourist areas. Sunset Watersports is one of the companies offering jet ski tours.

4 **Boating and Sailing**
The many dozens of marinas in the Keys are full of companies that are ready to rent you whatever kind of boat you would like – or to take you out, if that's what you prefer.

5 **Cycling**
There is no doubt that cycling is one of the best ways to see the Keys. The roads are fairly bike-friendly, especially in Key West, and bicycle rentals are readily available.

6 **Tennis**
Good tennis clubs can be found on just about every developed Key – on Islamorada at MM 76.8 bayside, Marathon at MM 53.5 oceanside, on Key West, of course, and elsewhere.

7 **Golf**
The Keys don't have as many courses as the rest of Florida, but there are several good ones, such as Key Colony Beach Golf, near Marathon, and Key West Golf Club, which is a more expensive option.

8 **Parasailing**
Sebago Watersports: www. keywestsebago.com
As close to growing wings as you can get, parasailing is easy, safe, and unforgettable. Many companies, such as Sebago, offer the experience.

9 **Windsurfing**
With prevailing winds and calm, shallow waters that remain so for miles out to sea, the Keys are ideal for windsurfing. Most busy beaches up and down the islands have shops that rent the necessary equipment.

10 **Snorkeling and Scuba Diving**
Since the Keys are almost entirely surrounded by America's largest living coral reef, the underwater world is one of the areas main treats.

Scuba diving on the reef, Key Largo

Special Tours and Events

1 Dry Tortugas
Key West Seaplane Adventures:
www.keywestseaplanecharters.com
A paradisical, undeveloped collection
of islands *(see p133)*, where the
snorkeling is unbeatable.

2 Key West Ghost Hunt
MAP A6 ■ Tours depart each
evening outside First Flight Restaurant
and Bar, 301 Whitehead St, Key West
■ www.ghosthuntkeywest.com
Discover the supernatural with a
90-minute stroll through the mysterious streets of Key West's Old Town.

**3 Bahama Village
Goombay Festival**
MAP A6 ■ Bahama Village, Key West
A celebration of Island culture and
life. Held in mid-October, it usually
merges with the Fantasy Fest.

Conch train outside Sloppy Joe's

4 Conch Tour Train
MAP A6 ■ 303 Front St,
Key West ■ 305 707 5775 ■ www.
conchtourtrain.com
Key West's train tour is a must-do
for first-time visitors. It gives an
overview of the place and all sorts of
insights into its history and culture.

**5 Old Town Trolley
Tour in Key West**
MAP A6 ■ 855 623 8289
■ www.trolleytours.com/key-west
Jump aboard this orange and green
trolley to see the sights of Key West.
A ticket for the narrated tour allows
you to hop on and off all day.

Fantasy Fest parade, Key West

6 Key West Fantasy Fest
MAP A6 ■ Last 2 weeks in Oct
■ www.fantasyfest.com
Held on Key West leading up to and
including Halloween, this is a festival
with a positive atmosphere *(see p75)*.

**7 Annual Conch-
Blowing Contest**
Early March is when this traditional
means of musical expression –
or noise-making in less-skilled
cases – fills the air over Key West.

**8 New Year's Eve
in Key West**
In Key West, welcoming the New
Year starts with the Last Sunset
celebration at Mallory Square,
followed by several local acts and
fireworks on Blackwater Sound.

9 Seven-Mile Bridge Run
MAP B6 ■ Late Mar–mid-Apr
■ Marathon Key ■ www.7mbrun.com
Enthusiastic runners take on the
Seven-Mile Bridge. The race has
been held every year since 1982 and
raises money for Marathon charities.

10 Hemingway Days
Held in the middle of the low
season, during the third week of July
(Ernest Hemingway's birthday was
July 21st), this party is most loved by
the locals, or "Conchs", who attend
in great numbers . Hemingway look-
alikes lead the celebrations and
tributes to the famous writer.

See map on pp120–21

Island Shopping

1 **Bésame Mucho**
MAP A6 ■ 315 Petronia St, Key West ■ www.besamemucho.net
This boutique, in the Bahama Village neighborhood, sells lovely gifts such as candles, jewelry, and home decor.

2 **The Gallery at Kona Kai Resort**
MAP C5 ■ MM 97.8 bayside, 97802 Overseas Hwy (US 1) ■ www.konakairesort.com
Impressive international artwork, including paintings by Sobran and Magni, powerful bronze sculptures, and fine Keys nature photography.

3 **The Shops at Mallory Square**
MAP A6 ■ 291 Front St, Key West
This 19th-century US Navy coal depot was converted into a two-level shopping center. It is now home to artisans, jewelry-makers, and gift stores.

African wood carvings, Archeo

4 **Archeo**
MAP A6 ■ 1208 Duval St, Key West ■ www.archeogallery.com
Rare African masks and wood carvings, plus stunning Persian rugs.

5 **Kino Sandals**
MAP A6 ■ 107 Fitzpatrick St, Key West ■ www.kinosandals.com
Sandal factory where every pair is an original design and handmade by artisans using natural leather uppers and natural rubber soles.

Kermit's Key West Key Lime Shoppe

6 **Kermit's Key West Key Lime Shoppe**
MAP A6 ■ 200 Elizabeth St, Key West ■ www.keylimeshop.com
This pretty little shop serves one of the tastiest Key lime pies in town, plus Key lime-flavor cookies, salsa, chutney, taffy, tea, and olive oil.

7 **Key West Aloe**
MAP A6 ■ 416 Greene St, Key West ■ www.keywestaloe.com
A company that has made their own all-natural products since 1971, without any animal testing.

8 **Tucker's Provisions**
MAP A6 ■ 611 Duval St, Key West ■ www.tuckersprovisions.com
Set in the center of Duval, this popular store is packed with all sorts of gifts unique to Key West, including hats, clothing, bags, wallets, and other accessories.

9 **Old Road Gallery**
MAP C5■ 88888 Old Hwy, Tavernier ■ www.oldroadgallery.com
Peruse beach-oriented artworks crafted by local artists at this pleasant gallery, sculpture garden, and pottery studio.

10 **Grand Vin**
MAP A6 ■ 1107 Duval St, Key West
If you are looking for great wines from around the world at good prices, and the chance to try many of them by the glass, this is the place. Sit out on the porch and enjoy.

See map on pp120–21

LGBTQ+ Venues

1 **Bobby's Monkey Bar**
MAP A6 ▪ 900 Simonton St,
Key West ▪ 305 294 2655
Lively, colorful gay bar popular with
both locals and visitors thanks to
its friendly staff and offbeat events.

2 **Saloon 1**
MAP A6 ▪ 504 Petronia St,
Key West ▪ Open 9pm–4am daily
Bawdy gay leather bar with a
scruffy but seductive atmosphere
and friendly bartenders.

3 **La-Te-Da**
MAP A6 ▪ 1125 Duval St,
Key West ▪ 305 296 6706
This upscale venue with an excellent
restaurant is a popular LGBTQ+ spot
with a hotel. "Guys as Dolls"
and other acts are performed in
the Crystal Room Cabaret nightly.

4 **Graffiti**
MAP A6 ▪ 721 Duval St,
Key West ▪ 305 295 0003
Expect trendy and pricey styles
at this store. Most of the fashions
are understated, but there's also
plenty of flash to suit the mood of
this fun island.

5 **Bourbon Street Complex**
MAP A6 ▪ 722 – 801 Duval St,
Key West
Included here are the Bourbon
Street Pub, the 801 Bourbon Bar,
Saloon 1, Pizza Joe's, and the New
Orleans House *(see p152)*. 801
features nightly drag shows.

6 **Gay Key West Visitor Center**
MAP A6 ▪ 808 Duval St, Key West ▪ 305
294 4603 ▪ www.gaykeywestfl.com
There's always plenty of information
here for the taking, as well as occasional meetings and social events.

7 **Aqua Night Club**
MAP A6 ▪ 711 Duval St,
Key West ▪ 305 916 1255
This vibrant club hosts a karaoke and
drag show. The poolside bar out back
is quieter, with torches and a waterfall. Happy hour from noon to 6pm.

8 **The Mermaid & The Alligator**
MAP A6 ▪ 729 Truman Ave, Key West
▪ 305 294 1894 ▪ www.kwmermaid.com
With lush gardens and posh
amenities, this elegant bed-and-
breakfast is LGBTQ+-friendly.

9 **Santa Maria Suites**
MAP A6 ▪ 1401 Simonton St,
Key West ▪ 305 296 5678
Located 3 miles (4.8 km) from
the airport and 8 minutes from the
beach, this classy resort is popular
with LGBTQ+ travelers.

10 **Island House Key West**
MAP A6 ▪ Atlantic Ocean
end of White St Pier
This popular gay resort *(see p152)* has
a palm-fringed pool, 24-hour poolside
bar, and a jacuzzi (clothing is optional).

Drag queen, Bourbon Street Complex

Bars, Pubs, and Clubs

Traditional saloon, Captain Tony's

1 Captain Tony's Saloon
MAP A6 ■ 428 Greene St, Key West

This was the original Sloppy Joe's, where Hemingway was a regular. Live bands feature; Conch hero Jimmy Buffett used to sing here.

2 Sloppy Joe's
MAP A6 ■ 201 Duval St, Key West ■ 305 294 5717

You can get a full meal as well as just a drink at this always noisy bar. It's heavy on Hemingway memorabilia, since he used to hang out here as well as at the original Sloppy Joe's.

3 Green Parrot Bar
MAP A6 ■ 601 Whitehead St, Key West ■ 305 294 6133

Established in 1890 and still going strong. Lots of locals, pool tables, and all kinds of live music on weekends.

4 Bull and Whistle Bar
MAP A6 ■ 224 Duval St, Key West ■ 305 296 4545

Three bars in one, on three different floors. Street level always has some live entertainment; the top floor deck houses the Garden of Eden (see p57), the famous clothing-optional bar.

5 Jimmy Buffett's Margaritaville
MAP A6 ■ 500 Duval St, Key West ■ 305 292 1435

Local-boy-made-good Jimmy Buffett is the owner of this bar-restaurant-souvenir shop. There is live music nightly, and on occasion the Parrot Head leader himself shows up.

6 Little Room Jazz Club
MAP A6 ■ 821 Duval St, Key West ■ 305 741 7515

Tune into some jazz while sipping delicious island cocktails at this mecca for music lovers. Gourmet grub pub, wine, and craft beers are also offered here.

7 Schooner Wharf Bar
MAP A6 ■ 202 William St, Key West ■ 305 292 9520

This bar is located in the Historic Seaport District, offering open-air views of the waterfront and live music.

8 Hog's Breath Saloon
MAP A6 ■ 400 Front St, Key West ■ 305 296 4222

Hog's Breath sign

One of the best-known bars in Key West, Hog's Breath was founded in 1988. Expect a traditional saloon bar setting, lots of heavy drinking, and live music.

9 The Rum Bar
MAP A6 ■ 1117 Duval St, Key West ■ 305 296 2680

Enjoy well-made island cocktails while relaxing on the wraparound porch, with lively people-watching opportunities. It is located inside the Speakeasy Inn.

10 Rick's Bar/Durty Harry's Entertainment Complex
MAP A6 ■ 202 Duval St, Key West ■ 305 296 4890

This large complex has eight bars, and Rick's upstairs is one of the hottest dance clubs in town.

See map on pp120–21

Conch Dining

PRICE CATEGORIES

For a three-course meal for one with half a bottle of wine (or equivalent meal), taxes, and extra charges.

$ under $35 ■ $$ $35–$70 ■ $$$ over $70

 A & B Lobster House
MAP A6 ■ 700 Front St, Key West ■ 305 294 5880 ■ $$$

Maine lobster, fresh shrimp, and waterfront views in a historic building.

2 Tavern N Town
MAP A6 ■ 3841 N Roosevelt Blvd, Key West ■ 305 296 8100 ■ $$$

Floribbean cuisine is served in the elegant surroundings of the Tavern N Town. Try the conch chowder.

3 Blue Heaven
MAP A6 ■ 729 Thomas St, Key West ■ 305 296 8666 ■ $$

Trademark Key West chickens and cats wander about in the garden of this wonderful Caribbean restaurant.

4 Mangoes
MAP A6 ■ 700 Duval St, Key West ■ 305 294 8002 ■ $$

Go not just for the exciting food (try the signature Key West loaded pineapple) but also because the place is so central to Key West life.

5 Louie's Backyard
MAP A6 ■ 700 Waddell Ave, Key West ■ 305 294 1061 ■ $$$

Enticing haute cuisine in an easy, breezy setting right on the Atlantic.

 Conch Republic Seafood Company
MAP A6 ■ 631 Greene St, Key West ■ 305 294 4403 ■ $$

Tuck into fresh seafood prepared in the traditional Conch Style. The venue also hosts daily happy hours and raging private parties.

7 Mangia Mangia Pasta Café
MAP A6 ■ 900 Southard St, Key West ■ 305 294 2469 ■ $$

Open only for dinner, this central Italian café has superb fresh pasta.

8 Sarabeth's
MAP A6 ■ 530 Simonton St at Southard, Key West ■ 305 293 8181 ■ $$

The fluffy omelets, Key lime pie French toast, and lemon ricotta pancakes make this a favorite for Sunday brunch.

9 El Siboney
MAP A6 ■ 900 Catherine St, Key West ■ 305 296 4184 ■ $

Great Cuban food in abundance in a no-nonsense setting. Lots of diversity, such as roast pork with cassava and tamale, or breaded *palomilla* steak.

10 One Duval
MAP A6 ■ Pier House Resort, 1 Duval St, Key West ■ 305 295 3255 ■ $$

The chef utilizes the abundance of ingredients indigenous to the Caribbean and the Florida peninsula, preparing them with a flourish that redefines regional cuisine.

Spectacular views from One Duval

TOP 10 Side Trips

If you venture out of the more touristed confines of Greater Miami, be ready for something quite different. The Everglades look and feel completely different to the coast, especially compared to glitzy South Beach, and even the Gulf Coast and Treasure Coast enclaves seem to exist in a world apart. Gone entirely is the international feel, and in its place is a sense of the old Florida.

Naples pier with the lovely pink sunset reflecting on the water

SIDE TRIPS

Top 10 Sights
see pp133–5

Places to Eat
see p136

Places to Stay
see p137

Dry Tortugas
from Key West

1 Fort Myers
MAP A2

Famous as the base of operations for the 19th-century inventor Thomas Alva Edison, Fort Myers is home to the Edison & Ford Winter Estates, which commemorates Edison and the motor car mogul Henry Ford. Other attractions include the family-friendly IMAG History & Science Center, the Caloosahatchee River, and Fort Myer's historic downtown. To the southwest, on Estero Island, is the Fort Myers Beach, known for its miles of sandy stretches.

2 Sanibel and Captiva Islands
MAP A3

The Lee Island Coast has irresistible sandy beaches, rare wildlife, lush vegetation, and wonderful sunsets. The jewels in the crown are the Sanibel and Captiva Islands, which have a Caribbean-style laid-back vibe mixed with upscale shops and restaurants. Much of the territory is protected, and development limited: there are a few high-rise hotels, and mainly just houses and cottages.

3 Dry Tortugas from Key West
MAP A5 ▪ Yankee Freedom: 800 634 0939

Travel to the wonderful islands of the Dry Tortugas by seaplane or ferry from Key West. The Yankee Freedom ferry company offers a daily trip. The day-long tours include food

and snorkeling gear. Camping overnight is also possible. The most visited island is Garden Key, the site of Fort Jefferson and its fantastic snorkeling beaches *(see p55)*.

Loxahatchee National Wildlife Refuge

4 Loxahatchee National Wildlife Refuge
MAP D3 ▪ 10216 Lee Rd, Boynton Beach ▪ 561 734 8303 ▪ Open 24 hrs daily ▪ Adm

This is the only surviving remnant of the northern Everglades, a vast area of mostly sawgrass marsh that is so characteristic of the Everglades environment. The inviting public-use areas provide viewing opportunities for a large variety of wetland flora and fauna, including egrets, alligators, and the endangered snail kite. Activities include nature walks, hiking, canoeing, bird-watching, and bass-fishing. A 5-mile (8-km) canoe trail provides the best way to see and explore the refuge up close.

5 A1A North along the Treasure Coast
MAP D2

If you continue on the A1A north of Palm Beach, the megalopolis gives way to the smaller, quieter towns of the Treasure Coast. These include Vero, the largest; Jupiter, which has no barrier islands; Stuart, with its charming historic district; rural-feeling Fort Pierce; and, at the northern extension of the Treasure Coast, the fishing village of Sebastian.

Fort Jefferson, Dry Tortugas

6 The Everglades, across the Tamiami Trail (Highway 41)
MAP A3–C4

Highway 41 was the first cut across the Everglades and from its inception has been called the Tamiami Trail, which stands for Tampa-Miami, the two cities it connects. However, it does take you into Seminole country, where you can experience the wonders of the Everglades *(see pp34–5)*. As you head to the Gulf Coast, stop at Everglades City and Naples.

City Hall, Everglades City

7 A1A North along the Gold Coast

Starting just at the northern tip of Miami Beach is a stretch of beautiful, wealthy communities that goes on for at least 50 miles (80 km). As diverse in their own ways as the Greater Miami area, they add immeasurably to the cultural richness of South Florida, and most offer large, enticing swathes of sand *(see pp30–31)*.

Beach hugging the Gold Coast road

8 Naples and Around
MAP A3

If you cross the Everglades, your inevitable first stop on the Gulf Coast will be Naples. An affluent beach city, Naples prides itself on its manicured appearance, 90 golf courses, and an elegant downtown area. There's a pleasant pier where you can commune with pelicans or do some fishing, and 10 miles (16 km) of pristine, sugary beaches, with warmer waters than the Atlantic Ocean. Nearby Marco Island, the most northerly of the Ten Thousand Islands archipelago, is a good base for delving into the western fringe of the Everglades. It has been the source of significant Calusa finds, some dating back 3,500 years.

9 Big Cypress Seminole Reservation
MAP B3–C3 ■ **Accessible from Rte 833 off the I-75**

Located on the northern border of the Big Cypress National Preserve, the largest Seminole reservation in the state of Florida is the best place to meet the locals and get some sense of the lives of the modern tribe. The main Seminole settlement can be found 15 miles (24 km) north of the I-75, and has a few basic diners and gift shops, as well as the illuminating Ah-Tah-Thi-Ki Museum *(see p34)*, where videos, a rare collection of clothing and artifacts, and exhibitions by Seminole artists highlight the history and cultural traditions of the tribe.

Alligator Alley in the Everglades

10 The Everglades, across Alligator Alley (I-75)

MAP B3–C3

This toll road across the Everglades keeps you at arm's length from the swampy, teeming mass. There are several great stops along the way, as you pass through Big Cypress National Preserve and north of Fakahatchee Strand State Preserve (see p35).

HURRICANE IAN

Hurricane Ian made landfall in September 2022, causing mass destruction across Florida and western Cuba. Buildings and infrastructure on Sanibel Island and the islands off Fort Myers were badly damaged. Many local establishments were forced to close their doors. While it is still worth visiting, you may notice extensive building work as the area attempts to recover.

A DAY TRIP ALONG THE A1A NORTH OF FORT LAUDERDALE

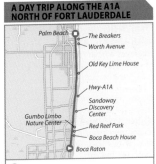

Palm Beach — The Breakers — Worth Avenue — Old Key Lime House — Hwy-A1A — Sandoway Discovery Center — Gumbo Limbo Nature Center — Red Reef Park — Boca Beach House — Boca Raton

▶ MORNING

Drive north along **Highway A1A** (see pp30–31) to ritzy Boca Raton, one of South Florida's wealthiest communities and sprinkled with 1920s Mediterranean Revival architecture by Addison Mizner. Stop at the **Gumbo Limbo Nature Center** (see p55), and stroll its mangrove forest boardwalks to watch for ospreys, brown pelicans, and the occasional manatee. Pop across to adjacent **Red Reef Park** (see p55) for sunbathing on the beach and swimming. Retrace your route south back to the Palmetto Park Road junction and turn right – a block on the right is local favorite **Boca Beach House** (887 E Palmetto Park Rd). Have lunch here.

AFTERNOON

Continue 9 miles (14 km) north on Highway A1A to the Sandoway Discovery Center in Delray Beach. In a 1936 beachfront house, exhibits include a butterfly garden, shell gallery, and coral reef pool with live sharks. Drive 9 miles (14 km) north before taking a left at Ocean Avenue for a pit stop at the **Old Key Lime House** (p77) in Lantana, a 19th-century throwback with great Key lime pies. End the day with a final 9 miles (14 km) along the A1A to Palm Beach (see p76), the island town known for its palatial homes and more Mizner Mediterranean-style architecture. Take in the plush shops along **Worth Avenue** (see p30), before cocktails at the opulent **Breakers** (see p30).

See map on p132 ←

Places to Eat

1 HaVannA Cafe
MAP B4 ▪ 191 Smallwood Dr, Chokoloskee ▪ 239 695 2214 ▪ $$

Located on Chokoloskee Island, this hidden gem combines classic Cuban cooking with fresh seafood.

2 Okeechobee Steakhouse
MAP D2 ▪ 2854 Okeechobee Blvd, W Palm Beach ▪ 561 683 5151 ▪ $$$

Old-fashioned steakhouse open since 1947, knocking out juicy bone-in rib eye and porterhouse steaks, as well as a celebrated coconut cream pie.

3 The Veranda
MAP A2 ▪ 2122 2nd St, Fort Myers ▪ 239 332 2065 ▪ $$$

Charming restaurant, with Deep South decor. The menu includes blue crab cakes, steaks, and salads.

4 Swamp Water Café
MAP C2 ▪ 30000 Gator Tail Trail ▪ 863 983 6101 ▪ $

The menu features classic traditional American dishes and Native American delicacies. Try the Indian taco or fry bread with honey butter.

5 Joanie's Blue Crab Café
MAP B4 ▪ 39395 Tamiami Trail E, Ochopee ▪ 239 695 2682 ▪ $

An old-fashioned seafood shack on the edge of the Everglades that is open for lunch most days.

PRICE CATEGORIES
For a three-course meal for one with half a bottle of wine (or equivalent meal), taxes, and extra charges.

$ under $35 $$ $35–$70 $$$ over $70

6 Rod and Gun Club
MAP B4 ▪ 200 W Broadway, Everglades City ▪ 239 695 2101 ▪ No credit cards ▪ $

In a classic Florida frontier hotel, with great views and fresh fish sandwiches.

7 Sinclair's Ocean Grill
MAP D2 ▪ Jupiter Beach Resort, 5 North A1A ▪ 561 745 7120 ▪ $$$

Traditional Floribbean food – a bit of Caribbean, Pacific Rim, and Floridian.

8 The Dock at Crayton Cove
MAP A3 ▪ 845 12th Ave S at Naples Bay ▪ 239 263 9940 ▪ $$$

For more Floribbean cuisine, head to The Dock to try the macadamia nut crusted snapper and Key lime grouper.

9 Keylime Bistro
MAP A3 ▪ 11509 Andy Rosse Lane, Captiva Island ▪ 239 395 4000 ▪ $$

Fun and funky, with a beachy feel. Try the tricolor vegetarian terrine.

10 MudBugs Cajun Kitchen
MAP A3 ▪ 1473 Periwinkle Way, Sanibel Island ▪ 239 472 2221 ▪ www.mudbugssanibel.com ▪ $$

A slice of the bayou on Sanibel, with live music and Cajun cuisine.

Bikes outside Joanie's Blue Crab Café

Places to Stay

 Trail Lakes
MAP B4 ▪ 40904 Tamiami Trail, Hwy 41, Ochopee ▪ 800 504 6554 ▪ www.evergladescamping.net ▪ $$

There are camping sites, cabins, and thatched-roof chickee huts. Amenities are extremely basic but allow you to experience the Everglades up close.

 Rod and Gun Lodge
MAP B4 ▪ 200 W Broadway, Everglades City ▪ 239 695 2101 ▪ No credit cards ▪ www.rodandguneverglades.com ▪ $

This place has a colorful past that includes stays by Hemingway, US presidents, and Mick Jagger.

3 Conrad Fort Lauderdale
MAP D3 ▪ 551 N Fort Lauderdale Beach Blvd ▪ 954 414 5100 ▪ $$$

The nautical-style decor of this hotel is second only to its ocean-front location. It offers superb ocean views, an elevated pool, and a tranquil spa.

4 Casa Grandview
MAP D2 ▪ 1410 Georgia Ave, W Palm Beach ▪ 561 655 8932 ▪ www.casagrandview.com ▪ $$

Set in the historic Grandview Heights district, this luxurious B&B offers romantic suites and breakfast on its beautiful veranda.

5 Jupiter Beach Resort
MAP D2 ▪ 5 North A1A, Jupiter ▪ 561 745 2511 ▪ www.jupiterbeachresort.com ▪ $$

The rooms are simple but have marble baths, colorful furnishings, and (mostly) terrific views.

6 Marriott Sanibel Harbour Resort and Spa
MAP A3 ▪ 17260 Harbour Pointe Dr, Fort Myers ▪ 239 466 4000 ▪ www.marriott.com ▪ $$

Spacious and light rooms, and a recreational area with a private beach.

PRICE CATEGORIES
For a standard double room per night (with breakfast if included), taxes, and extra charges.

$ under $200 $$ $200–$400 $$$ over $400

7 Island Inn
MAP A3 ▪ 3111 W Gulf Dr, Sanibel Island ▪ 239 472 1561 ▪ www.islandinnsanibel.com

Luxury inn that survived and rebuilt quickly after Hurricane Ian in 2022, with boutique studios and suites that have balconies overlooking the beach.

Suite at the Inn on Fifth

8 Inn on Fifth
MAP A3 ▪ 699 5th Ave S, Naples ▪ 239 403 8777 ▪ www.innonfifth.com ▪ $$$

Cozy hotel radiating Mediterranean charm, with lavish fountains.

9 Waterstone Resort & Marina
MAP D3 ▪ 999 E Camino Real, Boca Raton ▪ 561 368 9500 ▪ www.waterstoneboca.com ▪ $$$

On the shores of Lake Boca, this plush hotel offers easy access to watersports and waterside dining.

10 Clewiston Inn
MAP C2 ▪ 108 Royal Palm Ave, Clewiston ▪ 863 983 8151 ▪ www.redlion.com ▪ $

This charming inn evokes a pre-Civil War atmosphere with its decor.

See map on p132

Streetsmart

A busy street along Ocean Drive,
fringed by palm trees

Getting Around	140
Practical Information	144
Places to Stay	148
General Index	154
Acknowledgments	159

Getting Around

Arriving by Air

Most major international airlines serve **Miami International Airport**. The free MIA Mover links the airport with the Miami Intermodal Center, comprising the Rental Car Center and Miami Central Station (with bus and Metrorail services).

Taxis, ride shares, and **SuperShuttle** shared vans are available; charging according to a zone system.

Fort Lauderdale-Hollywood International Airport is the region's second airport. Broward County Transit bus No. 1 provides a cheap service to Fort Lauderdale, and there are free shuttles to the nearest Tri-Rail station at Dania Beach.

Although **Palm Beach International Airport** is much smaller, it serves many US and Canadian destinations. **Palm Tran** runs local bus service No. 44 into West Palm Beach, and there are free shuttles to the nearest Tri-Rail station.

Key West International Airport serves only a handful of US destinations.

Arriving by Sea

The **Port of Miami** is the busiest cruise ship hub in the world. It is accessible by car or taxi, though most cruise lines offer direct shuttle services to Miami International Airport.

Train Travel

Amtrak, the national passenger rail company, serves Florida from the east coast. There is one daily service from New York City. This Silver Service takes up to 28 hours, and runs via Washington D.C., down through Jacksonville and Orlando, terminating in Miami. Sleepers and meals are available on this journey. The Palmetto serves the same route and offers a business-class service.

If you want to travel by train to Florida but take your own car to drive once you get there, book a ticket on Amtrak's Auto Train, which runs daily from Lorton in Virginia to Sanford, Florida – 250 miles (400 km) north of Miami. The journey takes about 18 hours.

Amtrak also offers local train services around south Florida. Trains stop at several stations between Fort Lauderdale, West Palm Beach, and Miami Central Station.

If you are planning to make more than a couple of trips by train, it is worth buying a rail pass, which gives unlimited travel on Amtrak's network during a set period of time. The pass must be bought before you arrive – either online with Amtrak or through a travel agent that deals with Amtrak.

Another train service is the south Florida regional **Tri-Rail**, which links 17 stations between Miami airport and West Palm Beach, including Fort Lauderdale, Hollywood, Delray Beach, and Boca Raton. Although primarily for commuters, these trains can also be useful for visitors.

Long-distance Bus Travel

Whether you are traveling from other parts of the country or within Florida, **Greyhound** buses offer the cheapest way to get around. Some services are "express," with few stops en route, while others serve a greater number of destinations. A few routes have "flag stops."

There is a good, although fairly slow, service between Miami Central Station and Key West, as well as buses to Fort Lauderdale, West Palm Beach, and most coastal towns in between.

You can pay the driver directly but to reserve a ticket in advance visit the Greyhound website. You can also go to a Greyhound agent – usually found in a local store or post office.

Passes provide unlimited travel for set periods of time (between four and 60 days), but you may only find them particularly useful if you have a very full itinerary. Overseas visitors should also note that passes cost less if bought from a Greyhound agent outside the US.

Safety and hygiene measures, timetables, information about the different types of ticket, and details of baggage limits are available on the Greyhound website. **Red Coach** and **FlixBus** both run premium bus services all around Florida, most with reclining seats, on-board Wi-Fi and entertainment.

Public Transportation

Most South Florida cities only have bus networks, while Miami also has the **Metrobus**, **Metrorail**, and **Metromover**. Safety and hygiene measures, timetables, ticket information, transport maps, and more can be obtained at tourist information centers, stations, and individual operators' websites.

Tickets

You can get an EASY Ticket as a paper card or via the GO Miami-Dade Transit app. It can be loaded with top-up money and 1- and 7-Day Passes. Bus drivers also accept payments in cash using exact change. There are often discounted passes for multiple trips as well as reduced rates for children.

Bus

All of Florida's major cities have city bus networks. Metrobus runs throughout Miami-Dade County. A single ride costs $2.25 and transfers are free. A 24-hour unlimited pass costs $5.65, while a seven-day pass is $29.25. There is a 60 cent fee to transfer between bus and train services. You'll need the correct change, or a stored-value EASY Card or EASY Ticket, available at machines at the airport, any Metrorail station, or the Transit Service Center.

The free **Miami Beach Trolley** offers four routes running every 20 minutes 8am to 11pm daily. Routes include North Beach to Normandy Isle, 41st Street to Collins Avenue (Middle Beach loop), and the South Beach Trolley loop – with stops between 5th Street and Lincoln Road. The Collins Express trolley route links the Middle Beach and North Beach trolleys.

Metrorail and Metromover

Metrorail is a 25-mile (40-km) rail line that runs between the northern and southern suburbs of Miami. It provides a useful link between the most popular tourist areas of Coral Gables, Coconut Grove, the downtown area, and Miami airport. Services run daily every 10 minutes or so from 5am until midnight. To ride the Metrorail you must use an EASY Ticket. You can transfer free from Metrorail to the Tri-Rail line in Hialeah, and also to the Metromover system at Government Center and Brickell stations.

Metromover is Miami's free monorail. It has three loops, connecting the heart of downtown with the Omni entertainment and Brickell financial districts on separate elevated lines. There are 21 stations in total. The Inner Loop provides a quick way to see the downtown area. It operates from 5am to midnight daily, arriving every 90 seconds during rush hours and every three minutes during off-peak hours.

DIRECTORY

ARRIVING BY AIR

Fort Lauderdale-Hollywood International Airport
w broward.org

Key West International Airport
w eyw.com

Miami International Airport
w miami-airport.com

Palm Beach International Airport
w pbia.org

Palm Tran
w palmtran.org

SuperShuttle
w supershuttle.com

ARRIVING BY SEA

Port of Miami
w miamidade.gov/portmiami

TRAIN TRAVEL

Amtrak
w amtrak.com

Tri-Rail
w tri-rail.com

LONG-DISTANCE BUS TRAVEL

FlixBus
w flixbus.co.uk

Greyhound
w greyhound.com

Red Coach
w redcoachusa.com

PUBLIC TRANSPORTATION

Metrobus, Metromover and Metrorail
w miamidade.gov/transit

BUS

Miami Beach Trolley
w miamibeachfl.gov/city hall/transportation/trolley

Taxis

Taxis are a comfortable though expensive way of getting around. Cabs can be picked up at taxi ranks and hotels in larger city centers, as well as at airports. Most have a "TAXI" sign on the roof; this is illuminated if the taxi is free. They can also be booked by telephone or online. **Yellow Cab Taxis**, which operate in Miami, start at $2.95 for the first sixth of a mile, and $0.85 for each additional sixth of a mile until 1 mile. Then it's $0.55 per additional sixth of a mile. Ride-hailing apps also operate in the city.

Water Taxis

In Miami and Fort Lauderdale, local **Water Taxis** are a fun way to explore the area's 300 miles (482 km) of canals. Routes are generally geared to tourists, and as a result they are fairly limited in scope – linking hotels, restaurants, and stores, for example. However, it's great for sightseeing and often offers special fares.

Car Rental

Rental car companies are located at airports and other locations in major towns and cities. It is usually cheaper to rent a vehicle at the airport rather than from a downtown outlet.

All you need to rent a car is your driver's license, passport, and a credit card. If you present a debit card, you may have to pay a larger deposit. The minimum age for car rental is 21, but drivers under 25 may need to pay a surcharge.

The state of Florida requires that you carry a copy of the rental agreement in the car. It is recommended to store it safely out of sight.

Make sure your car rental agreement includes Collision Damage Waiver (CDW) – also known as Loss Damage Waiver (LDW) – or you'll be liable for any damage to the car, even if it was not your fault. Rental agreements include third-party insurance, but this is rarely adequate. It is advisable to buy additional or supplementary Liability Insurance, just in case.

Most companies add a premium if you want to drop the car off in another city, and all impose high charges for gas: if you return the car with less fuel than it had initially, you will be required to pay inflated fuel prices. Be aware that the gas stations nearest airports are particularly expensive.

Driving in Florida

Driving in Florida is an efficient way to get around urban areas and travel between cities. It's also very straightforward: most highways are well-paved, gasoline is relatively inexpensive, and car rental rates are among the lowest in the US.

While there are many state and federal regulations on the equipment requirements of cars, there are very few that pertain to occupants. You must have a valid driver's license, and drivers and passengers can be fined for not wearing seatbelts.

At certain times of the year state-wide campaigns make violations particularly expensive.

If you want to explore off-road trails on a motorbike, be aware that riders younger than 16 years are required to wear eye protection, over-the-ankle boots, and a safety helmet.

Parking

Finding a parking space is rarely a problem in Miami and the Keys, apart from near city beaches.

You will find small and multi-level parking lots or parking garages in cities, but usually you will have to use parking meters. Feed the meter generously: the fee varies from 50¢ to $2 per hour. Overstay and you risk a fine or the possibility of your car being clamped or towed.

Be sure to read parking signs carefully. Restrictions may be posted on telephone poles, street lights, or roadside walls. Cars parked within 10 ft (3 m) of a fire hydrant will be towed.

Roads and Tolls

Florida has an excellent road network. The fastest and smoothest routes are the interstate highways, which usually have six lanes and regular rest areas. They are referred to with names such as "I-10" and "I-75". Interstates form part of the expressway system of roads (sometimes called "freeways").

The major Interstates that lead to Miami are I95 down the north coast, and I75 from the Gulf Coast.

There is also Florida's Turnpike, which is a toll road shooting down from Central Florida. The toll you have to pay is dependent on the distance covered. Tolls can be paid to a collector in a booth or – if you have the correct change and do not need a receipt – dropped into a collecting bin. Note that most sections of the Turnpike have been converted to an electronic collection system and cash is no longer accepted. Tolls are collected via **SunPass** transponders or from having your license plate photographed at each toll booth; your rental car agency can provide information on this.

Other routes include the US highways, which are usually, but not always, multi-lane. These are slower than expressways and often less scenic, because they are lined with motels and gas stations. Highways 1, A1A, and 41 are not efficient unless you want to explore the Greater Miami area.

State Roads and County Roads are smaller but better for casual touring by car. Unpaved routes exist in some of Florida's more rural areas; note that some car rental companies may not permit you to drive on these.

Breakdown Assistance

If your car breaks down, pull off the road, turn on the emergency flashers, and wait for the police. On expressways you can make use of one of the Motorist Aid Call Boxes. If you have rented a car, you will find an emergency number on the rental agreement. The American Automobile Association (**AAA**) will assist its members. Alternatively, call the Florida Highway Patrol (511) or the Road Ranger service (*347).

Rules of the Road

Follow these rules to stay safe. Drive on the right-hand side of the road. Seat belts are compulsory for both drivers and passengers, and children under three must sit in a child seat.

Drinking and driving is illegal. Driving under the influence can result in a fine, having your driver's license suspended, or even imprisonment.

Passing is allowed on both sides on any multi-lane road, including interstate highways. It is illegal to change lanes across a double yellow or double white solid line.

If a school bus stops on a two-way road to drop off or pick up children, traffic traveling in both directions must stop. On a divided highway, only traffic traveling in the same direction need stop.

Cycling

Cycling is a good way to get around South Beach, Key Biscayne, and Key West, but is not recommended elsewhere in Miami or South Florida, where cars dominate. **CitiBike** has rental stations in Miami Beach, while **BikeMan Bike Rentals** offers eight locations in Key West.

For longer excursions there are miles of marked cycle paths along the coast, including the Florida Keys Overseas Heritage Trail runs along US–1 to Key West.

Walking

Miami is pedestrian-friendly and walking is one of the most enjoyable ways to get around. On foot, you can take in the architectural details, absorb the street life, and stop at any shop or bar that catches your interest.

Other Florida cities are not as walkable, especially in the hot and humid summers. But outside urban areas, the state has some lovely hikes. The **Florida Trail Association** provides information, including maps.

DIRECTORY

TAXIS

Yellow Cab Taxis
Ⓦ yellowtaximiami.com

WATER TAXIS

Fort Lauderdale Water Taxi
Ⓦ watertaxi.com

Miami Water Taxi
Ⓦ watertaximiami.com

ROADS AND TOLLS

SunPass
Ⓦ sunpass.com

BREAKDOWN ASSISTANCE

AAA
Ⓦ aaa.com

CYCLING

BikeMan Bike Rentals
Ⓦ bikemanbikerental keywest.com

CitiBike
Ⓦ citibikemiami.com

WALKING

Florida Trail Association
Ⓦ floridatrail.org

Practical Information

Passports and Visas

For entry requirements, including visas, consult your nearest US embassy or check with the **US Department of State**. All travelers to the US should have a passport that is valid for six months longer than their intended period of stay. Citizens of the UK, Australia, New Zealand, and the EU do not require visas for visits shorter than 90 days, but must apply to enter in advance via the Electronic System for Travel Authorization (**ESTA**). Applications must be made at least 72 hours before departure, and applicants must have a return airline ticket. Canadians will need a passport, but can travel throughout the US for up to a year without a visa or visa waiver. Visitors from all other regions will require a visa.

Government Advice

Now more than ever, it is important to consult both your and the US government's advice before traveling. The **US Department of State**, the **UK Foreign, Commonwealth & Development Office (FCDO)**, and the **Australian Department of Foreign Affairs and Trade** offer the latest information on security, health, and local regulations.

Florida is occasionally at risk from hurricanes. Advance warnings are activated if there is any danger and **Ready** lists safety precautions.

Customs Information

You can find information on the laws relating to goods and currency taken in or out of the US on the **Customs and Border Protection Agency** website. All travelers need to complete a Customs and Border Protection Agency form.

Insurance

We recommend that you take out a comprehensive insurance policy covering theft, loss of belongings, medical care, cancellations and delays, and read the small print carefully. All medical treatment is private and US health insurers do not have reciprocal arrangements with other countries.

Health

Healthcare in the US is excellent but costly. Ensure you have full medical coverage prior to your visit, and keep receipts to claim on your insurance if needed. Hospitals accept the majority of credit cards, as do most doctors and dentists. Those without insurance may need to pay in advance.

Most South Florida hospitals, such as **Coral Gables Hospital**, **Mercy Hospital Miami**, and **Mount Sinai Medical Center**, operate 24-hour emergency rooms, and there are a number of walk-in clinics for non-emergencies. The **Miami Urgent Care Center** is a dependable option in the city, while **Advanced Urgent Care** is recommended in Key West.

There are 24-hour drugstores such as **Walgreens** in most areas. Anyone on prescribed medication should take a supply with them to Miami and ask their doctor to provide a copy of the prescription.

There are few health hazards in Florida apart from mosquito bites, sunburn, and sunstroke. Wear hats and sunscreen, and drink plenty of water. Tap water is drinkable unless otherwise stated.

For information regarding COVID-19 vaccination requirements, consult government advice.

Smoking, Alcohol and Drugs

Florida has a partial smoking ban, with lighting up prohibited in most enclosed spaces and on public transportation. Users of e-cigarettes follow the same rules.

You must be over 21 to buy and drink alcohol, and to buy tobacco products. It is advisable to carry valid ID at all times, as you will not be permitted to enter bars or order alcoholic beverages in restaurants without ID.

The possession of narcotics is strictly prohibited and could result in prosecution and a prison sentence.

Personal Security

Florida is a relatively safe place to visit, but it is

still advisable to take precautions. As in any urban area, there are parts of Miami, and other Florida towns, where you should stay alert. Plan your routes in advance, look at maps discreetly, walk with confidence, and be cautious in deserted areas. If you need directions, ask hotel or shop staff, or the police.

Make sure your credit cards, cell phone, and cash are kept in a safe place. If you have anything stolen, report the crime as soon as possible to the nearest police station. Get a copy of the crime report in order to claim on your insurance. Most credit card companies have toll-free numbers for reporting a loss, as do Thomas Cook and American Express for lost cash cards.

Contact your embassy or consulate as well as the police if you have your passport stolen. In the event of a serious crime or accident, call the **emergency number**.

As a rule, Floridians are accepting of all people, regardless of their race, gender, or sexuality. The state has a big Latin American and African American population. Following the Black Lives Matter protests sparked by the killing of George Floyd in the summer of 2020, some confederate statues have been removed, and buildings and squares named after historical figures have been renamed.

Miami and the Keys have a long history as LGBTQ+-friendly vacation destinations. This attitude, however, does not always extend to the state's more rural areas. If you do feel unsafe, the **Safe Space Alliance** pinpoints your nearest place of refuge.

Travelers with Specific Requirements

US federal law demands that all public buildings be accessible to people in wheelchairs.

A number of groups offer general advice for travelers with disabilities, including **Mobility International USA** and Visit Florida *(see p147).* **Visit Florida Keys** provides island-specific advice and the **Florida Disabled Outdoors Association** lists recreational activities throughout the state.

When it comes to getting around, most city buses are able to "kneel" to make access easier – look for a sticker on the windshield or by the door. A few car rental companies, including **Wheelchair Getaways**, have vehicles that are adapted for people with disabilities.

DIRECTORY

PASSPORTS AND VISAS

ESTA
w esta.cbp.dhs.gov

US Department of State
w travel.state.gov

GOVERNMENT ADVICE

Australian Department of Foreign Affairs and Trade
w smartraveller.gov.au

Ready
w ready.gov/hurricanes

UK Foreign, Commonwealth & Development Office (FCDO)
w gov.uk/foreign-travel-advice

CUSTOMS INFORMATION

Customs and Border Protection Agency
w cbp.gov

HEALTH

Advanced Urgent Care
w urgentcareflorida keys.com

Coral Gables Hospital
w coralgableshospital.org

Mercy Hospital Miami
w mercymiami.com

Miami Urgent Care Center
w miamiurgentcare.com

Mount Sinai Medical Center
w msmc.com

Walgreens
w walgreens.com

PERSONAL SECURITY

Emergency Number
☎ 911

Safe Space Alliance
w safespacealliance.com

TRAVELERS WITH SPECIFIC REQUIREMENTS

Florida Disabled Outdoors Association
w fdoa.org

Mobility International USA
w miusa.org

Visit Florida Keys
w fla-keys.com/travelers-with-disabilities

Wheelchair Getaways
w wheelchairget aways.com

Time Zone

Miami and the Keys are in the Eastern Time Zone, five hours behind Greenwich Mean Time and three hours ahead of California.

Money

The currency is the US dollar ($), made up of 100 cents (¢). Bills (notes) come in denominations of $1, $5, $10, $20, $50, and $100, while coins are 1¢ (usually called a penny), 5¢ (nickel), 10¢ (dime), 25¢ cents (quarter) and, rarely, 50¢ (half-dollar), and one dollar.

Most establishments accept major credit, debit, and prepaid currency cards. Contactless payments are becoming increasingly common, but cash is usually required for smaller items, bus tickets, and tips. You should always tip service industry workers. Waiters and taxi drivers will expect to be tipped 15 per cent of the total bill, while hotel porters and housekeeping should be given $5 per bag or day.

Electrical Appliances

The standard US electric current is 110 volts and 60 Hz. Power sockets are type A and B, fitting plugs with two flat pins.

Cell Phones and Wi-Fi

Triband or multiband cell phones from around the world should work in the US, but your service provider may have to unlock international roaming. It is worth checking this with your provider before you set off.

Even if your phone does work you'll need to be particularly careful about the roaming charges, especially for data, which can be extortionate. It can be much cheaper to buy a US SIM card ($10 or less) to use during your stay (you can also buy micro-SIMs or nano-SIMs). Some networks also sell basic phones (with free minutes) for as little as $30 (no paperwork or ID is required). The main network providers are AT&T, Sprint, T-Mobile US, and Verizon.

To make any call in Miami, even next door, you must dial the 305 area code, but not the 1 before it. The **Directory Assistance** is a useful service for finding telephone numbers.

Free Wi-Fi is ubiquitous in Miami. Most hotels, hostels, and coffee shops offer Wi-Fi, and there are several Wi-Fi hotspots scattered throughout the city.

Postal Services

The **United States Postal Service** operates Florida's postal services. The most comprehensive post offices are Miami Beach Post Office on Washington Avenue and Key West Post Office on Whitehead Street. Stamps are sold in many drugstores, hotels, and grocery stores. All US domestic mail goes first class, and you should use airmail for any overseas mail. Rates are currently $1.45 for letters to all international destinations.

Weather

South Florida, with its tropical climate, is a year-round vacation destination. However, late spring and summer can be uncomfortably hot, with rain almost every afternoon.

Roughly one in ten of the hurricanes to occur in the North Atlantic hits Florida. The hurricane season runs from June through November, with the greatest threat of storms being from August through October.

Opening Hours

The majority of shops are open 9am–6pm Monday–Saturday and noon–6pm Sunday, but be aware that times can differ considerably between cities and rural areas. Most museums and tourist sights in South Florida and Miami are open daily, although they may close on either Monday or Tuesday. Many businesses and attractions close on federal and state holidays.

The COVID-19 pandemic proved that situations can change suddenly. Always check before visiting attractions and hospitality venues for up-to-date hours and booking requirements.

Visitor Information

The **Greater Miami CVB** runs both local and international offices, and a website. It offers maps and pointers on everything in the Greater Miami area, including the Keys and the Everglades. The **Miami Beach, Coral Gables, Coconut Grove, Fort Lauderdale, Key West**, and **Palm Beach Chambers of Commerce** also offer information. Over in Florida City, the **Tropical Everglades Visitor Association** offers tips on tours and walks, fishing and boating, diving and snorkeling.

The **Greater Fort Lauderdale CVB** offers travelers information about Fort Lauderdale, Hollywood, and the neighboring beach towns, while the **Palm Beach CVB** covers Boca Raton, West Palm Beach, and the Treasure Coast.

The staff at the **Monroe County Tourist Development Council** (the Florida Keys and Key West) know everything about the archipelago. They provide the best maps and top tips for getting the most out of every single mile marker along the way. For general tips, the **Visit Florida** website is worth a visit.

Discount cards can potentially save you a lot of money in Miami and the surrounding area, but it's important to check the small print and to be realistic about how much you'll use them – most cards only save money if they are used to the maximum extent. The **Sightseeing Day Pass** and **Go City** offer discounted admissions in Miami.

Local Customs

Tipping is an important custom in Florida, as in the rest of the US. Anyone who provides a service expects to receive a "gratuity," and this needs to be calculated in the price of things like meals, hotel stays, and taxi journeys.

Language

The official language of Florida is English, but parts of Miami are home to large Latin American communities, where Spanish is also spoken.

Taxes

The state sales tax in Florida is 6 per cent. Local authorities can add additional levies up to a maximum 2.5 per cent. Miami adds 1 per cent.

Accommodations

The accommodations in Miami and the Keys range from chain motels to plush resorts. An extensive list of accommodations can be found on the Visit Florida website. Room rates vary enormously depending on the time of year. During the high season (December to April) book rooms well in advance.

DIRECTORY

CELL PHONES AND WI-FI

Directory Assistance
☎ 411

POSTAL SERVICES

United States Postal Service
🆆 usps.com

VISITOR INFORMATION

Coconut Grove Chamber of Commerce
🆆 coconutgrove chamber.org

Coral Gables Chamber of Commerce
🆆 coralgables chamber.org

Fort Lauderdale Chamber of Commerce
🆆 ftlchamber.com

Go City
🆆 gocity.com

Greater Fort Lauderdale CVB
🆆 sunny.org

Greater Miami CVB
🆆 miamiandbeaches.com

Key West Chamber of Commerce
🆆 keywestchamber.org

Miami Beach Chamber of Commerce
🆆 miamibeach chamber.com

Monroe County Tourist Development Council
🆆 monroecounty-fl. gov/328/Tourist-Develop ment-Council-TDC

Palm Beach Chamber of Commerce
🆆 palmbeachchamber. com

Palm Beach CVB
🆆 thepalmbeaches.com

Sightseeing Day Pass
🆆 sightseeingpass.com

Tropical Everglades Visitor Association
🆆 tropicaleverglades.com

Visit Florida
🆆 visitflorida.com

Places to Stay

PRICE CATEGORIES

For a standard, double room per night (with breakfast if included), taxes, and extra charges.

$ under $200 $$ $200–$400 $$$ over $400

Luxury

InterContinental Miami

MAP P2 ■ 100 Chopin Plaza, at Biscayne Blvd ■ 305 577 1000 ■ www. icmiamihotel.com ■ $$
One of the finest hotels, with amazing views and fine dining. A Henry Moore sculpture adorns the lobby and the rooms sport lavish marble bathrooms.

The Mayfair at Coconut Grove

MAP G3 ■ 3000 Florida Ave, Coconut Grove ■ 800 433 4555 ■ www.mayfair hotelmiami.com ■ $$$
Set on the top of a shopping mall, this hotel has large suites with mahogany furniture, marble baths, and spacious balconies.

W Miami

MAP N3 ■ 485 Brickell Ave, Downtown Miami ■ 305 503 4400 ■ www. wmiamihotel.com ■ $$$
Much of this unique hotel was designed by American interior designer Kelly Wearstler, though some amenities, such as the huge swimming pool, are the work of Philippe Starck. Enjoy sophisticated modern cuisine at the hotel's ADDiKT restaurant.

1 Hotel South Beach

MAP S3 ■ 2341 Collins Ave ■ 305 604 1000 ■ www. 1hotels.com ■ $$$
The first outpost of this exclusive hotel chain opened in South Beach in 2015, blending luxurious accommodation with eco-conscious living. LED lights, reclaimed materials and recycled wood keys are used throughout.

The Biltmore

MAP F3 ■ 1200 Anastasia Ave, Coral Gables ■ 855 311 6903 ■ www.biltmore hotel.com ■ $$
A beautiful landmark (see p24), exuding the glamour of a bygone era and epicurean delights in the Fontana restaurant (see p67). Rooms are set up in the grand European tradition, and it has one of the world's largest hotel pools.

The Breakers

MAP D2 ■ 1 South County Rd, Palm Beach ■ 844 574 6046 ■ www. thebreakers.com ■ $$$
A Palm Beach landmark of the Gilded-Age tradition, whose decor evokes the Spanish Revival taste that Flagler brought to Florida in the 1890s.

EAST Miami

MAP N3 ■ 788 Brickell Plaza, Downtown Miami ■ 305 712 7000 ■ www. east-miami.com ■ $$
Plush hotel featuring rooms with a sleek Asian style and floor-to-ceiling windows. It is home to the Uruguayan restaurant Quinto.

Four Seasons Resort, Palm Beach

MAP D2 ■ 2800 South Ocean Blvd, Palm Beach ■ 561 582 2800 ■ www. fourseasons.com ■ $$$
The service here is first-class, from fresh fruit and orchids in your large room with sea view, to a town-car shuttle to and from downtown Palm Beach, and one of the best restaurants around.

Key West Marriott Beachside

MAP A6 ■ 3841 Roosevelt Blvd, Key West ■ 305 296 8100 ■ www.keywest marriott.com ■ $$$
This houses the justifiably popular Tavern N Town restaurant (see p131), and offers spacious rooms, a swimming pool, and a private beach.

Loews Miami Beach

MAP S3 ■ 1601 Collins Ave, South Beach ■ 305 604 1601 ■ www.loewshotels. com/miami-beach ■ $$
SoBe's biggest Deco tower is on a sandy beach. The property incorporates an outpost of New York's Lure Fishbar restaurant, a spa, and a stunning pool area.

Mandarin Oriental Miami

MAP P3 ■ 500 Brickell Key Dr ■ 305 913 8288 ■ www.mandarinoriental. com ■ $$$
Located on Brickell Key (Claughton Island), near the Port of Miami. The curved building means most rooms have an ocean view. Check the website for special rates.

The Ritz-Carlton, Fort Lauderdale

MAP D3 ▪ 1 North Fort Lauderdale Beach Blvd, Fort Lauderdale ▪ 954 465 2300 ▪ www.ritz carlton.com ▪ $$$

Overlooking the beach, this luxury hotel features a world-class restaurant, spa, heated infinity pool, and a state-of-the-art fitness center. It is also on the trolley line, which provides free transport-ation to Las Olas and other attractions.

Art Deco Hotels

Albion

MAP S2 ▪ 1650 James Ave at Lincoln Rd, Miami Beach ▪ 305 913 1000 ▪ www.rubell hotels.com ▪ $

This hotel is excellent value, considering the extreme chic that exudes from the cutting-edge restoration of this great Deco original. Be sure to check out the pool's peek-a-boo portholes.

Beacon South Beach

MAP S4 ▪ 720 Ocean Dr ▪ 305 674 8200 ▪ www. beaconsouthbeach. com ▪ $

Perfectly located in the center of Ocean Drive, this good-value hotel is a great choice. Its rooms blend Modern and Art Deco furnishings.

Avalon

MAP S4 ▪ 700 Ocean Dr ▪ 305 538 0133 ▪ www. avalonhotel.com ▪ $

Actually two hotels on opposite corners of 7th Street, these perfectly located Deco bon-bons are great value. Located in the middle of SoBe's most popular stretch, it

offers comfortable rooms and a complimentary continental breakfast.

Cardozo South Beach

MAP S3 ▪ 1300 Ocean Dr ▪ 786 577 7600 ▪ www. cardozohotel.com ▪ $

Built in 1939 by Henry Hohauser, this lovely boutique hotel is owned by Gloria and Emilio Estefan. The chic rooms flaunt an all-white decor scheme.

The Betsy Hotel

MAP S3 ▪ 1440 Ocean Dr, Miami Beach ▪ 844 539 2840 ▪ www.thebetsy hotel.com ▪ $$

This stylish beachfront hotel sits at the quiet end of Ocean Drive and bills itself as a "community artistic oasis." Designed by L. Murray Dixon, its 130 rooms are all luxury, some with balconies overlooking the iconic Art Deco district.

Delano South Beach

MAP S2 ▪ 1685 Collins Ave ▪ Closed for renovation ▪ $$

This ultra-luxurious Postmodern wonder is a SoBe gem. The original, rather austere white exterior gives way to the divine madness of Philippe Starck inside, along with hilarious Dali- and Gaudi-inspired designs. The very chi-chi Leynia restaurant is an Argentinean grill that is inspired by the flavors from Japan.

Essex House

MAP S4 ▪ 1001 Collins Ave ▪ 877 532 4006 ▪ www. essexhotel.com ▪ $$

Set near SoBe's nightclubs, the Essex

offers classic Art Deco luxury and detail. Guests aged 21 years and over have access to the pool and patio at the Clevelander, its sister property, next door.

The Tony Hotel South Beach

MAP R4 ▪ 801 Collins Ave ▪ 305 531 2222 ▪ www.thetonyhotel. com ▪ $$

Comfortable and stylish, its interiors are the work of the extremely talented fashion designer Todd Oldham. The Hotel is set in a landmark 1939 Art Deco building and qualifies as a SoBe work of art in itself.

Hotel Victor

MAP S4 ▪ 1144 Ocean Dr ▪ 305 779 8700 ▪ www. hotelvictorsouthbeach. com ▪ $$

Given a comprehensive makeover by designers Yabu Pushelberg, the Victor's original 1936 Art Deco features – elegant mosaics and a tropical mural by artist Earl LePan – are offset by designer furniture and a tank full of live jellyfish.

National Hotel

MAP S2 ▪ 1677 Collins Ave ▪ 305 532 2311 ▪ www.nationalhotel. com ▪ $$

This Art Deco hotel is one of the coolest places to see or be seen on South Beach. It houses one of the longest swimming pools in Florida which is 205 ft (62 m) in length, plus a great poolside cabana spa.

Viajero Miami

MAP S4 ▪ 1120 Collins Ave ▪ 786 519 3737 ▪ www.viajerohostels. com ▪ $

Formerly the Stiles Hotel, this hostel is set in an impeccably restored 1938 Art Deco edifice. There are private rooms and dorms with Tropical Deco decor, coworking spaces, and a pool bar.

The Leslie

MAP S3 ▪ 1244 Ocean Dr, Miami Beach ▪ 786 476 2645 ▪ www.lesliehotel. com ▪ $

This retro boutique hotel, with flamingo pink and ultramarine blue interiors is just a few steps from the beach and the night-life blitz. The Leslie's stunning rooftop pool and terrace complete its vintage South Beach vibe.

Resorts and Spas

Cheeca Lodge and Spa

MAP C5 ▪ 81801 Overseas Hwy, Islamorada ▪ 844 489 9664 ▪ www.cheeca. com ▪ $$$

A tropical island world with a wonderful beach, various pools, golf, tennis, nature walks, hot-tubbing, sport fishing, snorkeling, windsurfing, etc.

DoubleTree Resort & Spa by Hilton Hotel Ocean Point

MAP H3 ▪ 17375 Collins Ave, Sunny Isles Beach ▪ 786 528 2500 ▪ www. hilton.com ▪ $$

Right next to the ocean, this luxuriously landscaped hotel features a palm-lined waterfront pool and a spa. Enjoy the compli-mentary warm chocolate chip cookies.

Hawks Cay Resort

MAP B6 ▪ 61 Hawks Cay Blvd, Duck Key ▪ 305 743 7000 ▪ www. hawkscay.com ▪ $$

An exclusive Keys resort that offers fishing, an offshore sailing school, scuba diving, snorkeling, parasailing, kayaking, waterskiing, glass-bottom boat tours, and several other exciting activities.

InterContinental at Doral Miami

MAP F3 ▪ 2505 NW 87th Ave, Doral ▪ 305 468 1400 ▪ www.ihg. com ▪ $$

Offering both city and pool views, this plush hotel's luxurious rooms are all soundproofed. Dine at the on-site restaurant Blue Matisse, or enjoy a cocktail at the Nau Lounge.

Boca Raton Resort and Club

MAP D3 ▪ 501 East Camino Real, Boca Raton ▪ 855 874 6551 ▪ www. bocaresort.com ▪ $$$

Built by one of Florida's early visionaries, Addison Mizner, in 1926. A mix of Mediterranean styles and fabled luxury is every-where, right down to the marble bathrooms with original brass fittings.

Carillon Miami

MAP H2 ▪ 6801 Collins Ave, Miami Beach ▪ 866 800 3858 ▪ www.carillon hotel.com ▪ $$$

Located on its own long stretch of beach, this deluxe spa and wellness resort features one- and two-bedroom suites with floor-to-ceiling windows and sensational views.

Casa Marina, Waldorf Astoria Resort

MAP A6 ▪ 1500 Reynolds St, Key West ▪ 305 296 3535 ▪ www.casamarina resort.com ▪ $$$

The first grand hotel in Key West still shows its posh roots. There is an air of rev-erie that contrasts with the pace on the rest of the hec-tic island. The understated rooms offer water views.

Fisher Island Club

MAP H3 ▪ 1 Fisher Island Dr, Fisher Island ▪ 305 535 6000 ▪ www.fisher islandclub.com ▪ $$$

The billionaires who favor this remote private island love the exclusivity that it provides. Personal golf-carts let you toodle around the beaches, restaurants, clubs, etc. A free car ferry runs every 15 minutes, off the MacArthur Causeway.

Fontainebleau, Miami Beach

MAP H3 ▪ 4441 Collins Ave ▪ 800 548 8886 ▪ www.fontainebleau. com ▪ $$$

Built in the 1950s, this is one of the great Miami Beach hotels. Rooms are large, many with amazing views, and there is a luxury pool complex and a huge beachside spa.

JW Marriott Miami Turnberry Resort & Spa

MAP H1 ▪ 19999 W Country Club Dr, Aventura ▪ 305 932 6200 ▪ www. marriott.com ▪ $$

Very grand, with oriental carpets, marble, and acres of landscaped islands that encompass waterways, a golf course, tennis courts, private beach, and harbor. The feeling is welcoming, clubby, and very rich.

The Ritz Carlton, Key Biscayne
MAP H4 ▪ 455 Grand Bay Dr, Key Biscayne ▪ 305 365 4500 ▪ www.ritzcarlton.com ▪ $$$
Offering panoramic views of the Atlantic ocean, this is a grand hotel in every respect. It features chic interiors, two pools, a spa, a tennis center, and many restaurants including Lightkeepers, Rumbar, Dune Burgers, and Cantina Beach.

St. Regis Bal Harbour Resort
MAP H2 ▪ 9703 Collins Ave, Bal Harbour ▪ 305 993 3300 ▪ www.marriott.com ▪ $$$
Famed for its butler service, this lavish ocean-front property features two tropical pools, the St. Regis Spa, Greek restaurant Atlantikós, and access to a gorgeous white sand beach.

Guesthouses

Kaskades Hotel
MAP S2 ▪ 300 17th St, South Beach ▪ 305 763 8689 ▪ www.thekaskades hotel.com ▪ $
Right in the heart of SoBe action, this luxury inn has rooms that feature loads of plush extras for a fraction of the cost at larger hotels, such as marble wet rooms, steam enclave rain showers, and coffee makers by Nespresso.

Hotel St. Michel
MAP G3 ▪ 162 Alcazar Ave, at Ponce de Leon Blvd, Coral Gables ▪ 800 848 4683 ▪ www.hotel stmichel.com ▪ $
European-style inn built in 1926, during the Merrick

heyday (see p25). Each room is unique, accented by beautiful antiques.

Sea Spray Inn
MAP D3 ▪ 4301 El Mar Dr, Lauderdale-By-The-Sea ▪ 954 776 1311 ▪ www.seasprayinn.com ▪ $
This charming inn is tucked away in a small resort town 11 miles (18 km) north of Fort Lauderdale airport. Each of the 16 apartments offers a fully-equipped kitchen and modern bathroom.

South Beach Hotel
MAP S2 ▪ 236 21st St, South Beach ▪ 305 531 3464 ▪ www.southbeach hotel.com ▪ $
Fully restored historic Art Deco property, in a quiet neighborhood in the northern end of SoBe. The contemporary rooms are superb value, with chic art and furnishings.

Bars B&B South Beach
MAP Q4 ▪ 711 Lenox Ave, South Beach ▪ 305 534 3010 ▪ www.barshotel.com ▪ $$$
Stylish B&B a few blocks from the beach. The chic, modern rooms are in minimalist greys and whites, with splashes of color from contemporary artworks. Complimentary wine and cheese nightly.

Hotel Ocean
MAP S3 ▪ 1230 Ocean Drive, Miami Beach ▪ 844 319 3854 ▪ www.hotelocean.com ▪ $
Across from Lummus Park and the beach, this hotel offers comfortable rooms, a Peruvian crystal color therapy spa, two

Mediterranean restaurants, and doorstep access to Ocean Drive.

Deer Run on the Atlantic
MAP B6 ▪ 1997 Long Beach Rd, Big Pine Key ▪ 305 872 2015 ▪ www.deerrunontheatlantic.com ▪ $$$
On a pristine beach, this is an ecofriendly Caribbean-style home where leisurely breezes and seclusion prevail. Breakfast is served overlooking the ocean.

Grandview Gardens
MAP D2 ▪ 1608 Lake Ave, West Palm Beach ▪ 561 221 2191 ▪ www.grandview-gardens.com ▪ $$
Set on a quiet block amid tropical gardens, the renovated 1925 property features Spanish Mediterranean architecture, an outdoor pool, and period rooms.

Marquesa Hotel
MAP A6 ▪ 600 Fleming St, Key West ▪ 800 869 4631 ▪ www.marquesa.com ▪ $$
Constructed in 1884, the extravagant compound of four exquisitely restored Conch houses is now set amid lush greenery. All rooms and suites have marble bathrooms.

South Beach Plaza Villas
MAP S3 ▪ 1411 Collins Ave, South Beach ▪ 305 531 1331 ▪ www.south beachplazavillas.com ▪ $$$
Super-friendly and very laid-back, the place feels more like it's in the islands somewhere remote, yet you're just a block away from SoBe. The rooms have character, and there's a garden to relax in.

For a key to hotel price categories see p148

The Gardens Hotel Key West
MAP A6 ▪ 526 Angela St, Key West ▪ 800 526 2664 ▪ www.gardens hotel.com ▪ $$$
This plantation-style property is Key West's grande dame among guesthouses. Multiple buildings comprise the hotel, including Bahamian "eyebrow" cottages. All rooms have garden views and most have Jacuzzis.

LGBTQ+ Hotels

AxelBeach Miami
MAP S3 ▪ 1500 Collins Ave, Miami Beach ▪ 786 628 6362 ▪ www.axel hotels.com ▪ $
Keeping true to its 1940s roots, The AxelBeach Miami is welcoming and inclusive with facilities such as a lavish pool and Sky Bar overlooking the hip Washington Avenue.

Cabanas Guesthouse & Spa
MAP D3 ▪ 2209 NE 26th St, Wilton Manors ▪ 954 564 7764 ▪ www.the cabanasguesthouse. com ▪ $$
Set in Wilton Manors, Fort Lauderdale's burgeoning gay district, this boutique hotel has an all-male day spa, two pools, and a clothing-optional Jacuzzi amid lush gardens.

New Orleans House
MAP A6 ▪ 724 Duval St, Key West ▪ 305 293 9800 ▪ www.neworleanshouse kw.com ▪ $
This is the only all-male guesthouse set in Key West's party center. It has a clothing-optional sun-deck, a pool, and a 15-man hot tub. Make most of the complimentary daily happy hour, and free access to the drag shows at 801 Bourbon.

Worthington Resorts
MAP D3 ▪ 543 N Birch Rd, Fort Lauderdale ▪ 954 630 3000 ▪ www.the worthington,com ▪ $$
This resort is known as the largest all-male, clo-thing-optional resort in the country. Made up of three separate hotels, it offers three pools and two large hot tubs. Over-21s only.

Alexander's Guesthouse
MAP A6 ▪ 1118 Fleming St, Key West ▪ 305 294 9919 ▪ www.alexanders keywest.com ▪ $$
This carefully restored Conch house offers 17 comfortable guest rooms, a swimming pool and Jacuzzi, and a taste of tropical elegance. Breakfast is served poolside, and happy hour runs from 4:30 to 5:30pm.

Ed Lugo Resort
MAP D3 ▪ 2404 NE 8th Ave, Wilton Manors ▪ 954 275 8299 ▪ www.edlugo resort.com ▪ $$
Built from a series of renovated 1950s Florida bungalows, this LGBTQ+ resort is located close to the action of Wilton Manors. Adults-only, male exclusive, and clothing optional.

Equator Resort
MAP A6 ▪ 822 Fleming St, Key West ▪ 305 294 7775 ▪ www.equatorresort. com ▪ $$$
Clothing-optional men's resort in the core of Key West's primary gay district on historic Fleming Street. The resort's rooms are spacious and feature welcoming amenities.

The Grand Resort
MAP D3 ▪ 539 North Birch Rd, Fort Lauderdale ▪ 800 818 1211 ▪ www. thegrandresortandspa. com ▪ $$
An exclusive all-male spa-resort, just steps from the beach, with simple but comfy rooms. It has its own full-service day spa and hair studio, offering everything from a Swedish massage to a haircut.

Hôtel Gaythering
MAP Q2 ▪ 1409 Lincoln Rd, South Beach ▪ 786 284 1176 ▪ www.gay thering.com ▪ $
Ultrastylish and wildly popular hotel that offers teeny "crate shared rooms" (that come with sound machines), and larger king rooms decorated in a playful style. Extras include Miami Beach's only gay sauna and a stylish cocktail lounge.

Island House Resort Key West
MAP A6 ▪ 1129 Fleming St, Key West ▪ 305 294 6284 ▪ www.islandhouse keywest.com ▪ $$
Located in a quiet neighborhood, this all-male LGBTQ+ resort has tropical gardens, a pool, and two Jacuzzis. The bar offers happy hour daily between 5pm and 6:30pm.

Pineapple Point Guesthouse & Resort
MAP D3 ▪ 315 NE 16th Terrace, Fort Lauderdale ▪ 954 527 0094 ▪ www. pineapplepoint.com ▪ $$
Fort Lauderdale's premier accommodation for gay men resembles a tropical forest, with orchids, two hot tubs, and two pools.

Budget Accommodation

Beds N'Drinks

MAP S2 ▪ 1676 James Ave, Miami Beach ▪ 305 535 7415 ▪ www.beds ndrinks.com ▪ $

At the heart of SoBe, this hostel has private and shared rooms that vary from doubles to ten-bed dorms. They offer mixed and female-only dorms too. It has a patio and front terrace, a TV room, and VIP nightclub access.

Bikini Hostel

MAP Q3 ▪ 1255 West Ave, Miami Beach ▪ 305 253 9000 ▪ www.bikinihostel. com ▪ $

Choose between single or double rooms, and mixed or female-only dorms at this hostel. It features a beer garden, a pool, and ping-pong tables. The on-site café has breakfast, dinner, and bar food.

Freehand

MAP H3 ▪ 2727 Indian Creek Dr, Miami Beach ▪ 305 531 2727 ▪ www. freehandhotels.com ▪ $

This budget-friendly hotel has an outdoor terrace, a pool, two craft cocktail bars, and a restaurant. It offers a wide range of rooms including simple to stylish double rooms, and hip dorms with bunks that are equipped with privacy screens, power outlets, and reading lights.

Hollywood Beach Suites & Hotel

MAP D3 ▪ 334 Arizona St, Hollywood ▪ 954 391 9448 ▪ www.hollywood-beachsuitehotel.com ▪ $

The cheapest rooms here are a great deal, with sleek, modern furnishings, two bunks and space for up to six people. The property is just steps from the beach, where you can eat at the on-site Taco Beach Shack.

Hooseville Hostel

MAP E6 ▪ 20 SW 2nd Ave, Florida City ▪ 305 363 4644 ▪ www.hoosville hostel.com ▪ $

The incredible amenities include whimsical tropical gardens, a waterfall pool, TV lounge, tree house, fire pit, laundry facilities, a fully equipped kitchen, and a private bathroom.

The Julia

MAP R5 ▪ 336 Collins Ave, South Beach ▪ 305 497 7553 ▪ www.atmine hospitality.com ▪ $

This hotel in the First District of South Beach is just two blocks from the ocean. A budget-friendly property, The Julia's rooms are small, but smart and the rates include breakfast and happy hours.

Generator Miami

MAP H3 ▪ 3120 Collins Ave, Miami Beach ▪ 786 496 5730 ▪ www. staygenerator.com ▪ $

The Miami Beach branch of this boutique hostel chain offers slick private rooms and dorms, as well as a pool bar and taco restaurant. It rents bikes and skateboards, all one block from the beach.

Posh South Beach Hostel

MAP R4 ▪ 820 Collins Ave, Miami Beach ▪ 305 398 7000 ▪ www.posh southbeach.com ▪ $

As the name suggests, this is a "luxurious 5-star boutique" hostel, which in practice means designer bunk beds, plasma TVs, free fitness classes, a rooftop pool, and free-drink happy hours.

Seashell Motel & Key West Hostel

MAP A6 ▪ 718 South St, Key West ▪ 305 296 5719 ▪ www.keywest hostel.com ▪ $

Offers snorkeling trips and scuba instruction, plus bike rentals. It has a courtyard, picnic area, and game rooms, but only ten private rooms, so book in advance.

South Beach Rooms

MAP R4 ▪ 236 9th St, Miami Beach ▪ 305 399 9363 ▪ www.the hostelofmiamibeach. com ▪ $

Set in a great location, this resort is just two blocks away from the ocean. All rooms have air conditioning. You can choose between the spacious male- and female-only dorms, or the private rooms. There's also a TV room, a self-service kitchen, and an on-site luggage store.

Tropics Hotel and Hostel

MAP S3 ▪ 1550 Collins Ave, South Beach ▪ 305 531 0361 ▪ www. tropicshotel.com ▪ $

This is a genuine Art Deco building, complete with neon marquee. Though the rooms at Tropics are modest, the hotel's location on South Beach is unbeatable. There's even a pool.

For a key to hotel price categories see p148

General Index

Page numbers in **bold** refer
to main entries.

A
A1A 7, 11, **30–31**, 133, 134
Adrienne Arsht Center for
  the Performing Arts 60
Ah-Tah-Thi-Ki Seminole
  Indian Museum 34, 42, 75
Ah-Tah-Thi-Ki Swamp 34
Air travel 140
Alligator Alley 135
Amelia Earhart Park 58
Ancient Spanish Monastery
  38, 44, 57, 99, 101
Anhinga Trail 7, 34
Animals see Wildlife
Anis, Albert 17
Aquarium, Key West 58
Arch Creek Park and
  Museum 101
Architecture 40–41, 94
  Tropical Deco 14, **16–17**
Art Deco District 6, 10,
  14–17, 40, 77, 81, 83
Artspace/Virginia Miller
  Galleries 43
Art walks 73
Atlantis On Brickell 31,
  40
Audubon House & Tropical
  Gardens (Key West) 32
Audubon, John James 33

B
Bacardi Import
  Headquarters 41
Bahama Village (Key West)
  33, 41
Bahia Honda State Park 7,
  50, 54, 121, 124
Bal Harbour 99
Bankhead, Tallulah 33
Banks 146
The Barnacle 39
Barnacle Historic State Park
  (Coconut Grove) 108, 109,
  111
Barry, Dave 61
Bars: The Keys 130
Bartlett, Frederic and Evelyn
  31
Baseball 53
Basketball 53
The Bass 81
Bayfront Park 92, 94
Bayside Marketplace 6, 46,
  92, 94
Beaches 50–51, 73
  Bahia Honda State Park
    50, 121

Beaches (cont.)
  Beach at 12th Street
    (SoBe) 62
  Bill Baggs Cape Florida
    State Park 50, 82
  Crandon Park 50, 82
  Dr. Von D. Mizell-Eula
    Johnson State Park 7, 30
  Haulover Park Beach 51,
    62, 100
  Hobie Island Beach 50, 59
  Key West 50
  LGBTQ+ venues 62
  Lummus Park Beach 13, 51
  Matheson Hammock
    Park Beach 51
  South Beach 72
  South Pointe Park
    Beach 50
  Sunny Isles Beach 51
  Virginia Key Beach 50
Beacon Hotel 14
Beasley, Edmund 108
Bernice Steinbaum Gallery
  43
Big Cypress Seminole
  Reservation 134
Big Cypress Swamp 34
Big Pine Key 73
Bill Baggs Cape Florida
  State Park 50, 82
Billie, Chief Jim 39
Billie Swamp 34, 75
Biltmore Hotel (Coral Gables)
  6, 7, 24, 40, 107, 111
Biscayne Bay 6, 7, 59
Biscayne National Park 54,
  116
Boats 53, 59, 126, 140
Bonnet House 31
The Breakers 7, 30
Breakwater Hotel 14
Brickell, William 39
Brigade 2506 Memorial
  (Little Havana) 18, 38, 92
The Broadwalk 31
Broward Center 60
Budget travel 72–3, 153
Buffett, Jimmy 33
Buses 73, 141

C
Cafés 47, 88
Calle Ocho (Little Havana)
  10, **18–19**, 76, 92, 94
Calle Ocho Walk of Fame 6,
  19
Cape Florida Light 45, 59,
  83
Capitman, Barbara Baer 14,
  17, 39

Captiva Island 133
Cardozo Hotel 14, 83
Carnaval Miami 74
Cars 142–3
  see also Drives
Cavalier Hotel 15
Cemeteries: Key West
  Cemetery 32
  Woodlawn Park North
    Cemetery 19
Cernuda Arte 43
Charles Deering Estate 38,
  116, 117
Cher 61
Children's attractions 58–9
Chinese Village (Coral
  Gables) 25
Christ of the Abyss statue
  36–7
Churches
  Congregational Church
    (Coral Gables) 25, 40,
    111
  Ermita de la Caridad
    Church (Coconut
    Grove) 56
  Gesu Church 92
Clevelander 46
Clubs 13, 64–5, 87, 130
Coconut Grove 76, 108,
  109
  see also Coral Gables
    and Coconut Grove
Coconut Grove Arts Festival
  74
Coconut Grove Village 111
CocoWalk (Coconut Grove)
  47, 107
Collins Avenue 6, 13
Colony Hotel 14
Colony Theatre 60
Commodore Plaza 47
Conch dining 131
Congregational Church
  (Coral Gables) 25,
  40, 111
Coral Castle 38, 44, 104–5,
  115
Coral Gables and Coconut
  Grove 6, 7, **106–13**
  Coral Gables **24–5**
  maps 106–7, 109
  restaurants 113
  shopping 112
  special places and
    events 110
  walks, drives, and
    historic sites 111
Coral Gables City Hall 41
Coral Gables Merrick House
  38, 111

Coral Gables Museum 108
Corkscrew Swamp 34
COVID-19 146
Crandon Park 50, 82
Crane Point Museum and Nature Center 121, 124
Credit cards 146
Crime 144–5
Cruise ships 140
Cubans: Calle Ocho 92
  Cuban/Latino food 97
  Cuban/Latino shopping 96
  Cubaocho Museum 19, 42, 73, 92
  see also Little Havana
Cultural diversity 100
Currency 146
Customs and immigration 144
Custom House Museum, The 32
Cycling 52, 73, 84, 126, 143

D
David W. Dyer Federal Building 91
Deer 73
Deering, Charles 38, 39
Deering Estate see Charles Deering Estate
Deering, James 20, 21, 38, 39
Design District 100
Dewey, John 33
Diners 77
Dinner Key 109
Diving 54–5, 126
Dixon, L. Murray 17
Doctors 144
Dog racing 53
Dolphins 52, 121, 122, 123
Dominos Park 18, 92
Douglas, Marjory Stoneman 35, 39
Downtown and Little Havana 7, 90–97
  Cuban/Latino food 97
  Cuban/Latino shopping 96
  Latino arts venues 95
  maps 90–1, 93
  A trip through Calle Ocho 93
  walks and viewpoints 94
  see also North of Downtown
Drinks 65
Drives 76–7
  Coral Gables and Coconut Grove 111
  Downtown and Little Havana 94
  A tour of the Ancient Spanish Monastery 101
Driving licenses 142
Dry Tortugas 55, 133

Dr. Von D. Mizell-Eula Johnson State Park 7, 30
Dutch South African Village (Coral Gables) 25
Duval Street (Key West) 7, 32

E
Earhart, Amelia 109
Electrical appliances 146
Emergency services 145
Entertainers 61
Ermita de la Caridad Church (Coconut Grove) 56
Española Way 13
Essex House 15
Estefan Enterprises 40
Estefan, Gloria 14, 61
The Everglades 7, 11, 34–5, 76, 133–5

F
Fairchild, David 56, 109
Fairchild Tropical Botanic Garden 44, 48, 115
Fakahatchee Strand 34
Festivals 74–5, 110, 127
Fillmore Miami Beach at the Jackie Gleason Theater 61
Film Festival 74
Fink, Denman 24, 41, 91
Fishing 52, 84, 126
Flagler, Henry M. 30, 33, 39, 123
Flagler Museum 7, 30
Flamingo 35
Flamingo Gardens 48
Flamingo Park 81
Florida Keys Wild Bird Rehabilitation Center 123
Florida Pioneer (Coral Gables) 25
Fontainebleau Hotel 40
Food and drink 65, 67
  Cuban/Latino food 97
  see also Restaurants
Football 53
Forge Restaurant and Winebar 46–7
Forrester, Nancy 49, 57
Fort Lauderdale 30, 135
  LGBTQ+ venues 62, 63
Fort Myers 133
Fort Zachary Taylor Historic State Park (Key West) 33
France, Roy F. 17
Fredric Snitzer Gallery 43
Free events 72–3
Freedom Tower 40, 90
French City Village (Coral Gables) 25
French Country Village (Coral Gables) 25

French Normandy Village (Coral Gables) 24
Frost, Phillip 91
Frost, Robert 33
Fruit & Spice Park 45, 115

G
Gabriel Hotel 14
Gaínza, Agustín 92, 95
Galleries see Museums and galleries
"The Garden of Eden" (Key West) 57
Gardens see Parks and gardens
  Community Center (Key West) 63
  festivals 74
  hotels 152–3
  venues 62–3, 86, 129
Georgie's Alibi Monkey Bar 63
Gesu Church 92
Gleason, Jackie 61
Gold Coast 7, 11, 30–31, 133, 134
Gold Coast Railroad Museum 117
Golf 52, 84, 126
Government advice 144
Greynolds Park 101
Guadalajara 117
Guesthouses 151–2
Gumbo Limbo Nature Center 31, 55, 135
Gumbo Limbo Trail 7, 34

H
Haulover Park Beach 51, 62, 100
Health care 144
Hearst, William Randolph 38, 57, 99
Hemingway, Ernest 32, 33, 122
Hemingway Home (Key West) 7, 32, 123
Herzog & de Meuron 41, 91
Highway A1A 7, 11, 30–31, 133, 134
Hispanic Heritage Festival 75
Hispanic population 92
Historic sites and monuments 38–9
HistoryMiami Museum 43, 59
Hobie Island Beach 50, 59
Hohauser, Henry 14, 17
Hollywood Broadwalk 47, 76
Holocaust Memorial 38–9, 72
Horowitz, Leonard 14, 17
Horse racing 53

Hospitals 144
Hostels 153
Hotels 137, 147, 148–53
Hotel St. Michel 45
Hurricanes 117, 144, 146

I

Ice hockey 53
Indian Key Historic State Park 39, 122
Ingraham Building 40
In-line skating 52
Institute of Contemporary Art 73
Insurance 144
International Mango Festival 75
Internet 146
Islamorada 55
Italian Village (Coral Gables) 25

J

Jackie Gleason Theater 61
Jai alai 53
Jet-skiing 53, 84, 126
Jews
  Holocaust Memorial 38–9, 72
  Jewish Museum of Florida 42, 83
John Pennekamp Coral Reef State Park 54, 121, 124
Johnson, Don 61
Johnson, Philip 92
José Martí Park 19, 94

K

The Kampong 56, 109
Kayaking 53
Kevin Bruk Gallery 43
Key Biscayne see Miami Beach and Key Biscayne
Key Largo Hammock Botanical State Park 124
The Keys **120–31**
  bars, pubs, and clubs 130
  conch dining 131
  LGBTQ+ venues 129
  maps 120–1
  nature preserves 124
  shopping 128
  special tours and events 127
  sports 126
Key West 7, 11, **32–3**, 57, 122
  beaches 50
  maps 120, 123
  walk 123
  waters 54
Key West Butterfly and Nature Conservatory 58

Key West Cemetery 32
Key West Fantasy Fest 75
Key West Museum of Art and History 32
Key West Old Town 41, 77
Key West Tropical Forest & Botanical Garden 49
Kichnell & Elliot 17
King Mango Strut 75
Kite-flying 84
Kravis Center 60

L

Lapidus, Morris 40, 82
Las Olas Boulevard (Fort Lauderdale) 30
Latino arts venues 95
Leedskalnin, Edward 44, 115
Leslie Hotel 15, 83
LGBTQ+ travelers 13
Liberty City 75
Lifeguard Huts 12
Lighthouse Museum (Key West) 33, 123
Lignumvitae Key Botanical State Park 124
1111 Lincoln Road 41
Lincoln Road Mall 6, 12, 46, 73, 82
Little Haiti 75, 99
Little Havana 6, 7, **18–19**, 41, 55, 75
  see also Downtown and Little Havana
Little Havana Cigar Factory 6, 19, 92
Little Managua 75
Little Tel Aviv 75
Locust Projects 43
Long Key State Park 124
Looe Key National Marine Sanctuary 54, 124
Lopez, Jennifer 61
Lowe Art Museum 6, 7, 11, **26–7**, 43, 108, 111
Loxahatchee National Wildlife Refuge 133
Lummus Park Beach 13, 51
Lyric Theater 75

M

Madonna 61
Mahogany Hammock 7, 34
Mallory Square (Key West) 7, 32, 45, 47, 72
Malls and markets 70–1
Maps
  Art Deco District 15, 83
  beaches 50
  Calle Ocho, Little Havana 19
  chic shopping centers 68
  children's attractions 58

Maps (cont.)
  Coral Gables and Coconut Grove 106–7, 109
  Downtown and Little Havana 90–1, 93
  The Everglades 35
  exploring Miami and the Keys 6–7
  LGBTQ+ venues 62
  Gold Coast Highway A1A 31
  The Keys 120–1
  Key West 33, 120, 123
  malls and markets 70
  Merrick's Coral Gables Fantasies 24
  Miami and the Keys highlights 10–11
  Miami Beach and Key Biscayne 80–1, 83
  North of Downtown 98, 101
  off the Beaten Path 57
  parks and gardens 49
  romantic spots 44
  side trips 132
  snorkeling and diving 54
  South Beach 12
  South of Coconut Grove 114, 117
Margulies Collection 43
Marjory Stoneman Douglas Biscayne Nature Center 82
Markets 70–1
Martí, José 18, 33
Martin, Ricky 61
Matheson Hammock Park Beach 51
MDC Live Arts 95
Mel Fisher Maritime Museum (Key West) 33, 43, 122
Merrick, George 10, 24, 25, 38, 40, 44, 107, 108, 111
Merrick's Coral Gables Fantasies 10, **24–5**
Metromover 94
Miami Beach and Key Biscayne **80–9**
  LGBTQ+ venues 86
  Key Biscayne 54, 57, 76
  maps 80–1, 83
  nightlife 87
  restaurants 89
  shopping 85
  sidewalk cafés 88
  sports 84
  walks 76, 83
Miami Beach Botanical Garden 48–9
Miami Beach Post Office 41
Miami Children's Museum 58
Miami Circle 72
Miami-Dade County Auditorium 61

Miami-Dade County Cultural Center 92
Miami-Dade County Fair and Exposition 75
Miami Film Festival 74
Miami Tower 41, 92
Miami Vice 83
Miccosukee Indian Village 75
Miracle Mile (Coral Gables) 108, 115
Miracle Theatre 60
Mobile phones 146
Money 146
Money-saving tips 73
Monorail 141
Montgomery Botanical Gardens 49, 115
Morikami Museum and Japanese Gardens 48, 45
Multicultural attractions 75
Munroe, Commodore Ralph 108
Murals and mosaics 41, 72
Museums and galleries 42–3, 73, 146–7
  Ah-Tah-Thi-Ki Seminole Indian Museum 34, 42, 75
  Arch Creek Park and Museum 101
  Audubon House & Tropical Gardens (Key West) 32
  Barnacle Historic State Park (Coconut Grove) 108, 109, 111
  Bass, The 81
  Bonnet House 31
  Coral Castle Museum 104–5
  Crane Point Museum and Nature Center 121, 124
  Cubaocho Museum 19, 42, 73, 92
  Custom House Museum, The 32
  Flagler Museum 7, 30
  Fort Zachary Taylor Historic State Park (Key West) 33
  Gold Coast Railroad Museum 117
  Hemingway Home (Key West) 7, 32, 123
  HistoryMiami Museum 43, 59
  Jewish Museum of Florida 42, 83
  Lighthouse Museum (Key West) 33, 123
  Lowe Art Museum 6, 7, 11, **26–7**, 43, 108, 111
  Mel Fisher Maritime Museum (Key West) 33, 43, 122
  Miami Children's Museum 58

Museums and galleries (cont.)
  Museum of Contemporary Art North Miami 100
  Naomi Wilzig Erotic Art Museum 42
  Norton Museum of Art 30, 43
  Oldest House Museum (Key West) 73, 123
  Patricia & Phillip Frost Art Museum 116–17
  Pérez Art Museum 6, 7, 43, 91, 95
  Phillip and Patricia Frost Museum of Science 59, 91
  Stranahan House (Fort Lauderdale) 39
  Vizcaya Museum and Gardens 6, 7, 10, **20–21**, 38, 46, 107, 111
  Wolfsonian-FIU 6, 11, **28–9**, 42, 83

N

Nancy Forrester's Secret Garden (Key West) 49, 57
Naomi Wilzig Erotic Art Museum 42
Naples 134
National Key Deer Refuge 122
Native Americans 75
  Ah-Tah-Thi-Ki Seminole Indian Museum 34, 42, 75
  Arch Creek Park and Museum 101
  Big Cypress Seminole Reservation 134
  Indian Key Historic State Park 39, 122
  Lowe Art Museum 26
Nelson, Henry O. 17
New World Center 61
Nightlife 13, 64–5, 87, 130
Noguchi, Isamu 92, 94
North of Downtown **98–103**
  maps 98, 101
  restaurants 103
  shopping 102
  A tour of the Ancient Spanish Monastery 101
Norton Museum of Art 30, 43

O

Ocean Drive 13, 46, 83
O'Donnell, Rosie 61
Off the beaten path 56–7
Old City Hall 13
Oldest House Museum (Key West) 73, 123
Olympia Theater 60, 95
Opening hours 146

Outdoor activities 52–3
Overtown 56
Overtown Historic Villages 75

P

Palm Beach 30, 76, 135
Pancoast, Russell 17
Parasailing 53, 126
Parks and gardens 48–9
  Ancient Spanish Monastery Cloister and Gardens 44
  Arch Creek Park and Museum 101
  Audubon House & Tropical Gardens (Key West) 32
  Bayfront Park 94
  Bonnet House 31
  Fairchild Tropical Botanic Garden 44, 48, 115
  Flamingo Gardens 48
  Flamingo Park 81
  Fruit & Spice Park 49, 115
  Greynolds Park 101
  José Martí Park 19, 94
  The Kampong 56, 109
  Key West Tropical Forest & Botanical Garden 49
  Miami Beach Botanical Garden 48–9
  Montgomery Botanical Gardens 49, 115
  Morikami Japanese Gardens 45, 48,
  Nancy Forrester's Secret Garden (Key West) 49, 57
  Pinecrest Gardens 48, 58
  Vizcaya Museum and Gardens 6, 7, 10, **20**, 38, 44, 107, 111
Passports 144
Patricia & Phillip Frost Art Museum 116–17
Pei, I. M. 41, 92
People-watching 46–7
Pérez Art Museum 6, 7, 43, 91, 95
Performing arts venues 60–61
Personal security 144–5
Phillip and Patricia Frost Museum of Science 59, 91
Pigeon Key 123
Los Pinareños Fruteria 56
Plaza de la Cubanidad 18
Polevitsky, Igor B. 17
Police 145
Polo 53
Postal services 146
Poverty 100
Pride Center at Equality Park 62
Pubs 130
Pub Wilton Manors, The 62
Puente, Tito Jr. 61

R

Railroad Museum, Gold Coast 117
Railways 140, 141
Ramos, Roberto 92
Ramrod (Fort Lauderdale) 63
Red Reef Park 55, 135
Resort hotels 150–151
Restaurants 66–7
  budget travel 73
  Coral Gables and Coconut Grove 113
  diners 77
  The Keys 131
  Miami Beach and Key Biscayne 89
  North of Downtown 103
  side trips 136
  South of Coconut Grove 119
  see also Food and drink
Romantic spots 44–5
Rubell Museum 43

S

Safari Edventure 48, 115
Safety 144–5
Sailing 126
Sales tax 147
Sánchez Araujo, Antonio 92
Sanibel Island 133
Santería Botánica 56–7
Scuba diving 126
Shark Valley 7, 34
Shoppes of Wilton Manors 63
Shops at Merrick Park 111
Shopping 68–9, 147
  Coral Gables and Coconut Grove 112
  Cuban/Latino shopping 96
  Downtown and Little Havana 96
  The Keys 128
  malls and markets 70–71
  Miami Beach and Key Biscayne 85
  NOMA Beach at Redfish 119
  North of Downtown 102
  South of Coconut Grove 118
  souvenir shops 118
Side trips **132–7**
Skating, in-line 52
Skislewicz, Anton 17
Snorkeling 54–5, 126
SoBe see South Beach
Society of the Four Arts 41
South Beach (SoBe) 6, 10, **12–17**, 40, 72, 76, 81, 83
South Beach Wine and Food Festival 74
South Florida Land Rush 135

South of Coconut Grove **114–19**
  Deering Estate walk 117
  maps 114, 117
  restaurants 119
  souvenir shops 118
South Pointe Park Beach 50
Spas 150–1
Sports 52–5, 84, 126
Starck, Philippe 83
Stiltsville (Key Biscayne) 57
Stock-car racing 53
Stranahan House (Fort Lauderdale) 39
Sunny Isles Beach 51, 99
Sunset, Mallory Square 45, 72
Surfing 52, 84
Swartburg, Robert 17
Swimming 84, 126

T

Taberna del Pintor 92, 95
Tamiami Trail 35, 134
Taxes 147
Taxis 140
Teatro de Bellas Artes 95
Teatro 8 95
Telephones 146
Tennis 52–3, 84, 126
Theme parks:
  Amelia Earhart Park 58
The Tides 15
Time zone 146
Tipping 146, 147
Tourist information 146–7
Trains 140, 141
Travel 73, 140–43
Travelers with specific requirements 145
Treasure Coast 133
Trolley buses 141
Tropical Deco 14, **16–17**
Truman, Harry S. 33
Turtle Hospital 58
Tuttle, Julia 39

V

Venetian Pool (Coral Gables) 44, 107, 111
Versailles Restaurant 19, 67, 97
Viewpoints 94
Villa Casa Casuarina 12
Virginia Key Beach 50
Visas 144
Visitor information 146–7
Vizcaya Museum and Gardens 6, 7, 10, **20–21**, 38, 44, 107, 111
Vodou Botánica 56–7
Volleyball 52, 84

W

Waldorf Towers 14
Walks 76–7, 143
  Art Deco District 83
  Calle Ocho 92, 94
  Coconut Grove 109
  Coral Gables and Coconut Grove 111
  Deering Estate 117
  Downtown and Little Havana 94
Washington Avenue 6, 13
Water-skiing 126
Weather 117, 146
Welcome to Miami Beach Mural 41
Wertheim Performing Arts Center 61
Wildlife:
  Biscayne National Park 116
  The Everglades 34
  Florida Keys Wild Bird Rehabilitation Center 123
  The Keys 124–5
  Loxahatchee National Wildlife Refuge 133
  Marjory Stoneman Douglas Biscayne Nature Center 82
  National Key Deer Refuge 122
Williams, Tennessee 33, 122
Wilton Manors 63
Windley Key Fossil Reef State Geological Park 124
Windsurfing 52, 84, 126
Winter Party 74
Wolfsonian-FIU 6, 11, **28–9**, 42, 83
Woodlawn Park North Cemetery 19
Workouts 84
Worth Avenue (Palm Beach) 7, 30
Wyland Whaling Walls (Key West) 41
Wynwood Arts District 100
Wynwood Walls 43, 72, 100

Y

Yoga 73

Z

Zoos
  Key West Butterfly and Nature Conservatory 58
  Safari Edventure 48, 115

Acknowledgments

This edition updated by

Contributor Megan Eaves

Senior Editors Dipika Dasgupta, Alison McGill

Senior Designer Stuti Tiwari

Project Art Editor Ankita Sharma

Project Editor Alex Pathe

Assistant Editor Anjasi N.N.

Picture Research Administrator Vagisha Pushp

Picture Research Manager Taiyaba Khatoon

Publishing Assistant Simona Velikova

Jacket Designer Jordan Lambley

Senior Cartographer Subhashree Bharati

Cartography Manager Suresh Kumar

Senior DTP Designer Tanveer Zaidi

Senior Production Editor Jason Little

Senior Production Controller Samantha Cross

Managing Editors Shikha Kulkarni, Beverly Smart, Hollie Teague

Managing Art Editor Sarah Snelling

Senior Managing Art Editor Priyanka Thakur

Art Director Maxine Pedliham

Publishing Director Georgina Dee

DK would like to thank the following for their contribution to the previous editions: Hilary Bird, Toni DeBella, Susanne Hillen, Stephen Keeling, Jeffrey Kennedy, Patrick Peterson.

The publisher would like to thank the following for their kind permission to reproduce their photographs:

Key: a-above; b-below/bottom; c-centre; f-far; l-left; r-right; t-top

123RF.com: James Kirkikis 15tl, 10cla.

Alamy Stock Photo: age fotostock / Luis Castañeda 71tr, 94cla, / Alvaro Leiva 22-3, 76b; Walter Bibikow 18cla,130cb; Dennis Cox 4cla; Enigma 132ca; Jeff Greenberg 77tr, 89cla; 96tr; Chris Gug 55tr; Jeffrey Isaac Greenberg 4+ 42t; Jeffrey Isaac Greenberg 13+ 66t; Hemis.fr / Soularue 85tr; JOHN KELLERMAN 2tl, 8-9; Image Source 2tr, 36-7b; JeffG 71b; William S. Kuta 31crb; Maxine Livingston 48tc; Nikreates 108b; NiKreative 41cl; Sean Pavone 4crb; Red Square Photography / Corey Weiner 75tr; RosaBetancourt 11tc, 26cr, 53cl, 65cla, 69crb, 73tr, 88b, 101cla, 124b; Alex Segre 67cl; Stephen Saks Photography 11crb; Paul Thompson Images 62cla; VIEW Pictures Ltd / Dennis Gilbert 25cra; James Schwabel 18-19c, 34-35c; dov makabaw sundry 4clb; Robert Zehetmayer 3tl, 78-9; ZUMA Press 133cla.

The Ancient Spanish Monastery Museum & Gardens: 99tr.

Aventura Mall: Dana Hoff 69tl.

Big Pink: Gary James 86bc.

Books & Books: 110tl.

Courtesy of Vizcaya Museum and Gardens Archives: Bill Sumner 4cl, 10crb, 20ca, 20br, 21tl, 44t, 106cla, 111b.

Dreamstime.com: Allard1 15cr; Americanspirit 17c, 81t; John Anderson 76tl; Andylid 32-3, 130tl; Bennymarty 55b; Tony Bosse 58cl; Darryl Brooks 67tr; Buurserstraat386 45cra; Byvalet 82cl; Jillian Cain 116b; Coralimages2020 41tr; Brett Critchley 51tl; Songquan Deng 70clb; Tom Dowd 80cla; Dstaerk 4t; Russ Ensley 52tl; Fabio Formaggio 24-5; Fotoluminate 19bl, 40b, 52-3; Glen Gaffney 125bc; Giovanni Gagliardi 54cr, 56b, 118cla; Galinasavina 107br; Alex Grich-enko 40tc; Holocaust Memorial in Miami Beach, Florida, USA / photo Demerzel21 38bc; Wangkun Jia 14bl, 32cla; Stephen Kinosh 122tl; Kmiragaya 6cla, 18clb, 45bl, 53tr, 59br, 90cla, 94br; Daniel Korzeniewski 72tl, 92tl; Anna Krasnopeeva 15br; Lavendertime 82b; Mariakray 3tr, 138-39; Marynag 7br, 38t,115tr; Meinzahn 13tl, 14-5, 17b, 32br, 33cr, 47cl; Dmitry Mitrofanov 99b; Mramos7637 84cla; Sean Pavone 4b, 11ca, 16t, 30-1, 30bl, 104-05; Pitsch22 134cl; Luke Popwell 4cr,121cra; Romrodinka 50cl; Sborisov 114cla; Donnie Shackleford 49tr, Siegfried Schnepf 51b; Simonwehner 49crb; Smitty Smitty 34cl; Roman Stetsyk 12-3; Jeff Strand 57crb; TasFoto 31tl, 136b; Tinamou 10ca; Typhoonski 46b; Susan Vineyard 47tr; Viocara 113cr; Mirko Vitali 25br; Oleksandr Voloshyn 65tr.

Fairchild Tropical Botanic Garden: Jason Lopez 48b.

Florida Keys News Bureau: Bob Care 126b; Stephen Frink 54bl; Bob Krist 127cl; Andy Newman 75cl, 129b, 133bl; Rob O'Neal 127tr.

Getty Images: AFP Photo / Jeff Haynes 61tr; Walter Bibikow 116tl; Gustavo Caballero 102tl; Aaron Davidson 112b; Steven Greave 123cla; Jason Koerner 64b; The LIFE Images Collection / Ray Fisher 39tr; LightRocket / Roberto Machado Noa 71tr; Nicholas Pitt 107tl; mural by Serge Toussaint / photo Joe Raedle 98cla; Alexander Tamargo 64tl; Wirelmage / Thaddaeus McAdams 87cb.

Getty Images/iStock: 6381380 135tl, ablokhin 63br, 86tl; irabassi 125tr; Juanmonino 74b; Manakin 16cb, 60tl, 84br; ntzolov 77cl; Rauluminate 73cla; Serenethos 63t; TerryJ 11b.

Provided by the Greater Miami Convention & Visitors Bureau www.gmcvb.com: 42bl; Cris Ascunce19tl; Bruno Frontino 100cla; Human Pictures 39clb, 115bc.

Inn on Fifth: 137cr.

Jalan Jalan: 102bc.

Joe's Stone Crab: 89cb.

The Kampong: 109cl, Jon Alexiou 56tl.

Kermit's Key West Key Lime Shoppe: 128tr.

The Kravis Center: 60b.

Lincoln Road Mall: 12cl.

Mandolin Aegean Bistro: 103cra.

Miami Dade College: Cristian Lazzari 74cla.

Miami-Dade Parks and Recreation: Fruit & Spice Park 49cl.

Courtesy of National Park Service, Lewis and Clark National Historic Trail: 35tl.

New World Center: 61cl.

NOMA Beach: 119crb

Pérez Art Museum Miami: east façade February 2014, Designed by Herzog & de Meuron, Photo by Armando Colls/Mannyof Miami.com 95t; Daniel Azoulay Photography 43clb.

The Phillip and Patricia Frost Museum of Science: Ra-Haus 59t, 91tr.

Pier House Resort & Spa: One Duval 131b.

Pigeon Key Foundation: 122-3.

Robert Harding Picture Library: Richard Cummins 24bl; Gavin Hellier 134-5.

The Sanguich: 97cr.

Shutterstock.com: littlenySTOCK 1

South Miami-Dade Cultural Arts Center: Robin Hill 93bl.

SuperStock: age fotostock / Jeff Greenberg 34bl, 46tl, f/ Luis Fidel Ayerves 117cla; Richard Cummins 10cl; LOOK-foto 13br.

University of Miami Lowe Art Museum: Myrna and Sheldon Palley Pavilion for Glass and Studio Arts 26cla.

The Wolfsonian - Florida International University: 29crb, World Red Eye 83tl; The Mitchell Wolfson Jr. Collection / Wrestler (1929) by Dudley Vaill Talcott 28bl, / Window grille (1929) Architects: William Harold Lee and Armand Carroll 29tl, / Armchair (1931) by Edwin L. Lutyens 42c, /.Dressing table (1929) designer Kem (Karl Emanuel Marn) Weber 11cra, / Stained glass window, (1930) by Harry Clarke 28cr, / Ceiling and Chandeliers (1925-26) Robert Law Weed architect 28cla.

Courtesy of Wynwood Walls: Martha Cooper 43tr, 72b; Damian Morrow 100-1.

Cover

Front and spine: Shutterstock.com: littlenySTOCK

Back: **Alamy Stock Photo:** Ian Dagnall tr, Tasfot crb; **iStockphoto.com:** jfmdesig cl, jonnyse tl; Shutterstock.com: littlenySTOCK b.

Pull Out Map Cover

Shutterstock.com: littlenySTOCK.

All other images © Dorling Kindersley. For further information see: www.dkimages.com

Commissioned Photography Max Alexander, Peter Wilson.

First edition created by Blue Island Publishing

Penguin Random House

First edition 2005

Published in Great Britain by
Dorling Kindersley Limited
DK, One Embassy Gardens, 8 Viaduct
Gardens, London SW11 7BW, UK

The authorised representative in the EEA is
Dorling Kindersley Verlag GmbH. Arnulfstr.
124, 80636 Munich, Germany

Published in the United States by
DK Publishing, 1745 Broadway, 20th Floor,
New York, NY 10019, USA

Copyright © 2005, 2023 Dorling
Kindersley Limited
A Penguin Random House Company

23 24 25 26 10 9 8 7 6 5 4 3 2 1

A CIP catalog record is available
from the British Library.

A catalog record for this book is available
from the Library of Congress.

ISSN 1479-344X
ISBN 978-0-2416-2490-6

Printed and bound in Malaysia

www.dk.com

As a guide to abbreviations in visitor information blocks: **Adm** = admission charge.

MIX
Paper | Supporting
responsible forestry
FSC™ C018179